SHADOWS:
A Northern
Investigation of
The Unknown

Steve Cliffe

Published by Sigma Leisure – an imprint of
Sigma Press, 1 South Oak Lane, Wilmslow, Cheshire SK9 6AR, England.

British Library Cataloguing in Publication Data
A CIP record for this book is available from the British Library.

ISBN: 1-85058-369-2

Typesetting and Design by: Sigma Press, Wilmslow, Cheshire.

Cover illustration: Steve Cliffe and Dave Edwards

Printed by: Manchester Free Press

General Disclaimer

Whilst every effort has been made to ensure that the information given in this book is correct, neither the publisher nor the authors accept any responsibility for any inaccuracy.

Preface

Europeans regard the English as, "a people who see ghosts," according to that eminent Yorkshire sceptic, J.B. Priestley. It is a singular oddity of our race, he insisted, defying rational explanation, this fascination with the unknown.

To the European, the island of Britain is an off-shore perplexity, hidden by sea mist, guarded by legend and populated by fierce tribes. To the ancient Anglo-Saxon, who crossed the narrow seas to colonise a new land to the West, the sea was, "the path of audacity." And audacity it was indeed, as, moving inland, our forefathers encountered the deserted and crumbling ruins of Roman buildings – temples, villas and whole towns, silent and empty, the haunt of the crow and jackdaw, smothered and bearded in climbing ivy, treasuring secret echoes of vanished life.

When the Saxons built their wooden homesteads they avoided the Roman sites, believing them haunted by the dead of a strange race, who worshipped alien gods. These folk memories of another, earlier, people – "Th' Owd Man", as Derbyshire lead miners called the spirit of a pre-historic miner, reputed to haunt their diggings – lingered among the Celts also. Pushing far into the West, they encountered the remnants of very ancient peoples – some probably were the descendants of the megalith builders, who understood the purpose of eery burial chambers and stone circles which still dot the landscape.

Irish legend tells of the defeat of the Tuatha De – who were banished to rule an underground kingdom. These rulers of the underworld became identified as the "little people", or fairies, who populated magic castles in the green burial mounds. Flint arrowheads, used by neolithic peoples, are still described today as "elf bolts" in some regions of Britain. And there are even older race memories, of mythical monsters inhabiting the depths of still lakes or lonely mountain tops. Christianised, these folk memories were translated into devils and demons – fears born of dangerous wild beasts, the bear, the wolf, the wildcat, or of ancient rituals and tribal totems of the horned animal.

We do not have far to look. Almost every human habitation has its tale. Our journey will take us across Northern Britain, in the path of the ferry-man, in the direction of the dying sun.

Steve Cliffe

ACKNOWLEDGEMENTS

The author would like to acknowledge the opportunity to quote from the works of C.G. Jung and the permission given by Routledge for extracts, from "Synchronicity – an acausal connecting principle" and from the "Collected Works of C.G. Jung", published by Routledge and Kegan Paul, reproduced in this book.
I am also indebted to the Huddersfield Daily Examiner for permission to reproduce photographs and to their deputy chief photographer, Bob Staniforth, who took the excellent pictures.
I must thank Mark Mathews, a keen local historian, who took the interior shots of Dr Robinson's tomb – he is a brave man!
Stockport Libraries and Museums Service must be thanked for permission to use pictures of local interest. The British Museum supplied the picture of Lindow Man.
I reserve special thanks for my wife, Jean Cliffe, whose encouragement and analysis was provided at every stage of the book's preparation free of charge. But my warmest acknowledgement goes to Mr John Oldham, folklore expert, to whom this book is dedicated.

Tachraidh sinn fhathast
JOHN
Until we meet again

Contents

1

PEOPLE WHO SEE GHOSTS

The people who see ghosts – who are they? What are they like? As a reporter I have encountered and interviewed many such people. I should say, on superficial scrutiny, they all appear to be ordinary people, from various walks of life, of varying temperament and attitude. One thing they have in common is that they were not thinking of ghosts when they saw them.

The Society for Psychical Research has a very sophisticated system for cataloguing and classifying types of phenomena, and the persons reporting them – even down to psychological attitude type. The problem any serious investigator faces is the tendency possessed by all human beings to what psychologists call suggestion. Suggestion may occur before, or after, a psychic experience. If before, it operates as a trigger for the experience itself, if after, it can be due to exaggeration of the original experience and embellishment, which a questioner should try to avoid by letting the person tell their own story.

The case of Harry Martindale, the York policeman who saw the Roman ghosts, is an excellent example of how the pitfalls of the latter were avoided. He was first questioned by a Roman military expert, before he knew anything of Roman military dress and equipment. His unprompted descriptions confirmed what is historically known of the dress and weapons of Roman auxiliary soldiers – of which he had never read a line. His own knowledge of Romans was based on Hollywood epics not correlating to his actual experience. As he said: "Why me? I wasn't interested in ghosts or Romans."

Some ghost "stories" are just that. I remember once being called to a "haunted" restaurant in Huddersfield. It was a cold misty morning, and the restaurant, in an old Georgian building of Pennine stone, was full of disturbed cleaners and kitchen staff. The manageress was away, and the staff had definitely felt a strange presence following them down the twisting stair to the basement kitchen, brooding in the dining room – moving knives and forks only just laid, and even vigorously shaking an ornamental plant by the window. They became quite excited in their description of the events, but, unfortunately, not one had been present when the other had their "experience". When the story was published (newspapers will publish anything that more than one person insists upon) one reader was unkind enough to suggest in a letter to the editor that "the presence" was none other than the boy from the Boy and Barrel pub next door, who quit the chilly roof for the warm interior of the restaurant! The boy was a figure fixed on the roof as part of the pub sign. All I can add is that when the office Christmas party was held in the self-same restaurant, the only spirit present came out of bottles.

Bramall Hall, a black and white Cheshire mansion, holds dark secrets

Does a murdered serving-girl haunt Bramall Hall? Psychic investigator Angela Conway ponders the mystery.

Before we "pass-on" to graver accounts, and still on the subject of people who don't see ghosts, or rather only feel, or think they hear "something" – this is a salutary tale of amateur spook sleuths. Spook sleuthing has its hazards, as I know, having spent freezing nights in haunted Halls. On the whole I preferred the mountain. The chiming clocks kept me awake indoors.

Whilst engaged on a historical research project on old buildings, some colleagues of mine became intrigued by the allegedly inexplicable happenings at an old black and white timber-framed Hall, once belonging to the hereditary Serjeants of Macclesfield Forest, whose heraldic emblem was a felon with a noose around his neck – signifying their power of life and death over any who transgressed the forest laws. The descendants of this delightful family, some time in the nineteenth century, still bearing the magisterial powers, and no doubt upholding family tradition, were said to have covered up a domestic scandal involving the murder of one of their own maids in the servants quarters, by a member of the family. Contemporary records provide no evidence, but tradition asserts the foul deed was done, the victim having admitted the assailant into her quarters via a roof light in an apparently accustomed manner suggestive of the usual goings on. She was then battered, strangled and dragged across the room, thus providing a very tasty problem for the family to square with their Victorian consciences. Goodness knows how they solved it.

Staff at the Hall in recent days had been disturbed by the sound of footsteps in a wood-panelled room when no-one could be found to account for it, and there was the inevitable "cold spot" on the bare and neglected wooden stairs leading to the dusty and disused servants quarters, which induced a sense of fear approaching paralysis in some people, while others didn't notice it at all. The idea of a "ghost" hunt arose spontaneously among my colleagues.

To begin with, Bramall Hall, is part of Stockport Museums Service, and contains antiques and pictures of value. It is electronically wired up like Fort Knox, and the intrepid trio of Mark, Sarah and Diane, were reduced to kipping in the security room with the video surveillance equipment, instead of roaming whither the spirit took them. The caretaker, in his quarters across the corridor, did not stir all night. About 2 a.m., Diane, the more alert of the spook hunters, was surprised to hear the sound of a bolt sliding back, somewhere in the building. She adjusted the audio equipment, and listened horrified as footsteps began a regular tread across the floor.

Hurrying to rouse Sarah, so that she too could witness the ghostly tread, she discovered that the early hours are not the best time to alert certain persons to psychic activity. Sarah shrieked and burying her head in the sleeping bag refused to come out. Mark, much more sensibly, refused to wake up at all, and slept blissfully throughout the experience. As he explained to me later, in simple, manly terms: "These ghost hunts sound all right beforehand. But when people start getting excited over little bits of noise, I thought, best thing to get your head down and go to sleep!"

The caretaker was no help, and provided no explanation for the mystery. So was it central heating pipes, ancient oaken floorboards creaking, or the ghostly tread of a distracted murderer, wringing the hands that had lately wrung a neck?

Some psychic happenings defy explanation, while others, which begin with promise, end in farce.

Among the crop of persons convinced they had poltergeists abroad in the house after seeing *The Exorcist*, was one family I was told about, with a teenage daughter. They knew from watching the film that the eery phenomena usually revolved around a young person, and they became quite apprehensive when every time their daughter took a bath, an incredibly obnoxious smell pervaded the entire house, seemingly emanating from the bathroom. A personal hygiene problem being ruled out, they called in a professional exorcist to sanctify the premises and get rid of whatever was responsible for the appalling stench. He enthusiastically did the entire house, and the girl as well, for good measure. But the problem was not resolved, if anything the smell got worse. A psychic investigator heard of the case, and began a careful examination of the house, before long, solving the mystery.

The daughter, it seemed, was in the habit of reading in the bath for anything up to a couple of hours – longer than any other member of the household took in their ablutions. What the psychic investigator found was a light-shade – not possessed by the devil, but made of plastic, probably in Hong Kong, and inclined to emit a hideous odour on the adjacent light bulb becoming sufficiently hot to affect it. This only occurred when the teenage daughter of the house took her extended literary baths.

A promising story of a haunted house came to me via Bob Staniforth, a press photographer, and longtime collaborator of mine in ghost hunts. He heard of a house which had been empty since the owner had committed suicide by hanging himself, and the locals said they had seen strange lights, and moving shadows, when on-one was supposed to be there. What's more, the address was Gallows Green!

The owner had been a doctor, in a small town outside York. The house was an unremarkable '30s or '40s detached, facing onto the main York-Tadcaster road, and with its rear gardens abutting a housing estate of smaller semi-detached houses with views of the rear of the house. The doctor had been a Nigerian, and apparently developed distressing tendencies whilst resident in the house, his wife left him, and he subsequently hung himself. Not very mysterious until one considers the name of the place – Gallows Green – and the fact that in former times it was the custom to execute felons, by hanging, on the very spot.

What happened to the doctor? And was his suicide as straightforward as it seemed? Bob and I called on the people who live nearby, and asked them about the lights. Their evidence was vague and inconclusive. The lights may have been candles – moving from room to room, or possibly car headlights, on the main road beyond, reflected through from the front of the house, and casting strange shadows as they moved along. People show understandable reluctance to speak too freely of the recently dead. Moving lights, or corpse candles, as they are sometimes called, were widely regarded in Ireland and other places as warnings of imminent death. What they are, or how they operate no-one knows – but in what more suitable place could they be found, than one where so many had met a violent end? On Gallows Green.

Real ghost stories always have something extra – some inexplicable correlation with known fact which makes them that little bit more intriguing, and difficult to explain. And usually a pattern emerges – sometimes little-known sensations of phenomena, experienced by the people who report the happening, or something which they could not have known, fitting in with former facts. I am reminded of the haunting of the Cock and Bottle, a York city pub on Skeldergate, and how Mrs Brenda Stanley, picked out the face of the Duke of Buckingham from six other portraits she was shown, without knowing that his town-house had once stood on the site of her pub, or that he was an alchemist, who sought, among other things, the secret of immortality. She knew that his was the face that haunted her waking and sleeping hours, and that he, "wanted to get her". More later.

So who are the people who see ghosts? Probably as many and varied as the people who read this book. Why do people read ghost stories? You tell me.

2

THE GHOST WITH A BODY

Many pubs have ghosts. They are good for conversation, drum up casual trade, and even merit the occasional write-up in the local press. Any good landlord will be happy to tell you about the bumps and rattles, the guard dog who won't go into the beer cellar, the hand pumps that go on and off of their own accord, and the "inexplicable" disappearance, and reappearance of kitchen cutlery.

This pub was different. It not only had a ghost – it also had a body! Sceptics can check appropriate newspaper cuttings in the local library. They will get no other confirmation, because the place doesn't exist anymore. I once sent a research assistant to look for it, who simply got lost – and no wonder, because it's in the middle of a new motorway, and the unfortunate young man was on foot. Had his map reading been any more accurate, Paul might have become ghost number two.

Anyway it isn't a case of the sad disappearance of a pub so much as the strange re-appearance of a body, occasioned by the disappearance of the pub.

The Duke of Clarence was an old Regency Inn, built in about 1820, with a cheerful white stucco exterior. It's interior had interesting bar room features – such as the gentlemen's saloon, from which women were excluded in Victorian times, and screened from the rest of the pub, so that wives, in search of errant husbands, could not disturb their serious deliberations. It also had a chair, with wooden arms and back, about the same age as the pub, to which was fixed a brass plate bearing the legend "Old Joe". No-one knew to whom this name plate referred, but it was said of this chair, that patrons who sat in it for any length of time would be over come with an increasing sense of unease, so much so, that few cared to sit in it at all. Other people imagined they had seen a shadowy shape in the corner of the pub where the chair normally resided, when no-one was there. What is definitely attributed to the chair, by the former landlord, was an incident involving a cleaner. While polishing the chair one day, alone in the bar, before opening time, this unfortunate lady cried out, and dropped her duster. Reg, the landlord rushed into the room, thinking someone was trying to raid the till, but found the bar deserted, except for the cleaner and himself. "What's the matter?" asked Reg. "It's the chair," gasped the woman. Reg looked, and there was the chair, looking brown and battered as usual, but otherwise quite empty, upright, and not unusual. "So"? he enquired. "While I was dusting it someone touched me!" cried the woman. And she could never again be induced to clean the chair, on account of which it began to look even more neglected and forbidding.

The Duke of Clarence public house, Stockport, was long thought to have a ghost; when it was demolished, a skeleton was found bricked up in the cellar.

The regulars thereafter referred to "Old Joe" as if he were present, and would even enquire if he wanted a drink, and ask if he took spirits. Such fun came to an end when the pub was closed down, prior to its demolition to make way for the new motorway by-pass. Among the articles which were carried out and sold was Old Joe's chair. It was sold to an antique dealer, who very soon came to regret her purchase.

The demolition continued apace soon after, and it was when the level of the beer cellars were reached, that a very odd discovery was made. There were vaulted arches in these cellars, and one of them was bricked up, and inaccessible. When the diggers smashed through the intervening wall they discovered a crouching form, which on close examination turned out to be a skeleton, wearing a long greatcoat, and with an old-fashioned pair of Victorian style button-up boots lying nearby. The police were called, and the remains taken away for forensic examination. This established that the skeleton was of a man of middle years, but the remains were too badly deteriorated to determine the cause of death. An inquest was opened, but soon adjourned for lack of evidence. Judging by the clothing found, the date of death could have been anywhere between the late Victorian period and the beginning of this century.

Portwood – the district in which the Duke of Clarence was situated, had once been a populous residential area, with courts of back-to-back housing, dating from Georgian times. In this overcrowded area, with its cellar dwellings and communal loos, and one up one down homes, lived the poor working classes of the town. It had seen better days, when only a century before, it comprised the stately parkland of more affluent citizens. Now a development area, given over to industry and motorway, it is devoid of residents, but some of these transported to greener pastures, by an act of the council, were quick to remember old mysteries and feuds, when the macabre find prodded their recollections.

They flooded the local paper with theories as to the identity of the skeleton – they had been told the story by their mothers, their grandfathers, and so on. A favourite held the victim to be an Italian immigrant, who had been stabbed during an argument after a game of cards. His murderer had fled to America, and died in the great San Fransisco earthquake of 1906. Another had him as one of two brothers who fell out, and the murderer pushed him into an old brick kiln, on the spot, sealing the entrance. There had apparently been brick kilns somewhere in the vicinity of the pub, but whether they were connected to the beer cellars of the Duke of Clarence remains unknown. A more mundane explanation of the skeleton was that a tramp, finding a way into the cellars/brick kiln, from outside, had climbed in for shelter, and passed away in the course of the night from exposure – thus explaining why the shoes had been removed (or does it?). Either way the Duke of Clarence, in addition to having an alleged ghost, had a very definite skeleton, but the mystery of how it got there, or who it was, remains unsolved.

The chair inscribed "Old Joe" meanwhile, had been borne off in jubilation by the antique dealer – along with various other furniture, "for a song". Something more than that was exacted however, when a series of personal calamities afflicted the lady. Within days of the purchase her fiancé was arrested as an illegal immigrant, and despite dubious evidence, was held in prison for six months, and eventually deported, although impressive representations had been made on his behalf. This ill luck, the lady attributed directly to he acquisition of the chair, which she got rid of by rather inconsiderately passing it off cheaply on another dealer – which should give antique hunters pause for thought. Whether the ill-luck followed it we don't known. But quite possibly, somewhere, someone is unwittingly sitting on a chair with a mysterious brass plate inscribed "Old Joe". Maybe you will be offered the chair cheaply – the brass plate may even have been removed ...

3

DANGEROUS GHOSTS

From one pub called after a Duke, we go to a pub haunted by a Duke.

The Cock and Bottle, Skeldergate, York, was the scene of mysterious manifestations. It is on the site of a mansion owned by the 17th century Duke of Buckingham, who experimented with alchemy to try to achieve immortality.

For many years, this pub, the Cock and Bottle, Skeldergate, in York, was on the itinerary for a "Ghost Tour" organised by the appropriately named travel firm of Boswell and Johnson. I first came across it when following up several promising sites, suggested by the tour, for a newspaper article.

The then licensees were Peter and Brenda Stanley. Brenda was a quite lovely lady, with (when I saw her) blonde hair, an attractive figure, and, at the time, a slightly dreamy otherworldly manner. I remember she was about forty, with a pale pink rinse in her blonde hair, and wearing the latest fashion boots in knee-length black leather. It was quite clear that she believed the story she told of her experiences with an uncanny presence. At the time, however, I had reservations.

The Cock and Bottle is a good-sized modern pub, reconstructed from an older hostelry, the Plumber's Arms, and incorporating old timbers and stonework, which create an atmosphere of age where little exists.

Duke of Buckingham

Formerly the site was occupied by a townhouse, belonging to the second Duke of Buckingham, during the second half of the seventeenth century. It has good regular custom, both day-time and evening, because of its city location, and has no desperate need of passing trade, drawn by tales of itinerant ghosts.

Former licensees claimed they had heard a heavy door being forced open, when there was nothing to account for it, and an indistinct figure in a wide-brimmed hat was seen at a table. A sense of evil was said to pervade the place, sometimes freezing people to the spot, and sudden falls in temperature have been noticed. It was said the presence seemed to object strongly to the wearing of crosses and crucifixes.

In an interview with York historian and author, John Mitchell, Mrs Stanley said that since she and her husband moved into the pub just before Christmas in 1973, the strange occurrences had continued. She had seen the figure of a man with long dark hair, in various parts of the premises, and felt he might be seeking her help. Pictures had fallen from walls, doors had opened mysteriously, or locked themselves, and small objects disappeared, only to reappear in odd places. Also a mysterious skeleton had been discovered, buried on the spot where Buckingham had his library.

I interviewed Mrs Stanley, with my photographer friend, Bob Staniforth, in a wood-panelled corner of the pub, one starry November evening in 1975. First of all, she told us that she didn't believe the stories of a ghost when she first came to the pub. Then she told us what changed her mind.

"I was sitting watching television upstairs in the lounge. I must have sensed something, because I turned round. Then I thought I saw a shadow cross the television, and I saw another movement. It wasn't solid at all. I could see his shoulders, and long black wavy hair. He had a lump on the end of his chin, and a large nose. One eye was bigger than the other. Once I realised it was a ghost I was really frightened. I asked: 'What do you want?' He smirked at me, and just disappeared through the wall."

Although she knew the inn was haunted , Brenda had no idea who the ghost might be, until she was shown six pictures of old notables of York. She identified one as definitely that of her "visitor" – it was the 2nd Duke of Buckingham, George Villiers, whose mansion had once stood of the site of the modern pub.

She told Bob, and I, that "the Duke" regularly overlooked her during sleep. "I can feel him staring at me in the night, when I'm asleep – I had it last night. I'm not scared of him normally – but I'm sure that he knows during the night he does scare me. I feel that he's annoyed. I know he's trying to get me," she said finally.

Sometimes, while sitting at the bar, she had felt him touch her on the arms. There was a cold – "like a deep freeze cold," which seemed to go from person to person in the bar. Several times Mrs Stanley had come down and switched the light on in the bar, yet it had remained "dim and dismal". Tape recordings had been interfered with, the volume having been turned up and down, without human intervention. And sometimes Mrs Stanley said she could "hear him".

"I think he's attracted to me. He knows I like him, because he doesn't harm me." Brenda seemed a little uncertain on this point.

She showed Bob and I a brass plate, on the mantelpiece over a fire in the bar. She had placed it there, she told us, to hide a face she could make out in the stones on the chimney piece – because it looked like him
...

The stone she indicated revealed nothing to Bob or myself. It seemed bland and devoid of any but stone-like features, and more than anything else she said, this inclined me to consider her insight fanciful. However, as a disquieting postscript to this feature, years later, my wife, Jean, and I, visited the Cock and Bottle, and pointing out the alleged feature, which I had assured her was indiscernible, I was surprised to discover no difficulty in making out a face in the centre of a large stone, and my wife spotted it almost immediately, as I faltered in my denunciation, the brass plate having been removed by a new licensee.

"Well does it look like the Duke of Buckingham?" I enquired, my wife having perused his features. "Yes it does," she said. I could not be so positive, but there was certainly a face in the stone for those who looked for it – no longer hidden from view by an interposing brass plate, but open to the light of day.

So who was the Duke of Buckingham, and what was there about him to account for the strange happenings at the Cock and Bottle? To ask that in the days of Charles II would have been equivalent to asking who Margaret Thatcher, or some equally famous person, is nowadays. His father had been the political favourite of both James I and Charles I. George Villiers had grown up in the same nursery as the royal offspring, the later-to-be Charles II and James II. He was the special boyhood friend of Charles, and this friendship lasted throughout their lives, through varieties of fortune.

When Charles was in exile, in Paris, Buckingham arrived, and was blamed for introducing the young prince to, "all the vices and impieties of the age." He also introduced Charles to his tutor, Thomas Hobbes, a mathematician with views on politics and philosophy, which were said to influence the young man for the rest of his life.

Buckingham was witty and gay (in the old sense), and loved a boisterous life of hunting, drinking, arguing, and intriguing for power. His particular love was women, and he never got enough of them.

Born on January 30th, 1628, he was an Aquarian, that inventive and unpredictable sign – his judgments were often wide of the mark. He squabbled with Charles over the command of the army, when the Scots invaded England to try to regain the throne for the King from the English Parliament, who had declared a Republic.

When the expedition, and subsequent schemes were a failure, Buckingham blamed Charles' incompetence, when the main reason had been well-placed Parliamentary spies in the Royalist camp.

Soon after, he quit the weary world of exile, returned to England, and married Mary Fairfax, the daughter of a leading Parliamentarian, Lord Fairfax, a Yorkshire landowner, and former Lord General of Parliament's army. But he was not trusted, and Parliament stuck him in the Tower. It was not the last time he would be there, and he whiled away the time by building a laboratory, and conducting chemical experiments.

He was released in 1659, on security of £20,000 from Lord Fairfax, who he subsequently paid back by being scandalously unfaithful to the old man's daughter.

At the Restoration of Charles II, he bore the orb at the coronation of the King, and became a gentleman of the bed-chamber, and privy councillor. He was also made Lord Lieutenant of Yorkshire, and his restored estates brought in an annual income of £26,000, making him the richest man in England. In 1663 he successfully put down an insurrection in the county, and at the fall of Clarendon in 1667 he became the king's chief minister, and leader of the cabal which ruled the country.

His talent for erratic behaviour never deserted him. During a debate in the House of Lords, he punched a fellow peer, knocking the noble Lord's periwig off, while his assailant tore out a handful of Buckingham's hair. Both were forced to make a public apology for their indiscreet brawling.

He made up a poem about his rival in the cabal, Lord Arlington, which ran: "Two goggle eyes, so clear, tho' very dead, that one may see thro' them, right thro' his head!" A talent for satire made him many enemies in politics, and he was not a good leader of factions – "wanting to possess power, but not knowing how to use it."

He killed the Earl of Shrewsbury in a duel – although it took the Earl two months to die of his wounds. It had been fought because Buckingham was philandering with Shrewsbury's wife, and when Shrewsbury died, Buckingham quit his own wife, and lived openly with the Countess of Shrewsbury, who bore him a child. This was too much for Parliament, even in the days of relaxed morality associated with the Restoration, and Charles had to sack him.

Opinions as to his courage varied. Although an accomplished swordsman, and not averse to duelling when it suited him, he was accused of more frequently giving offence than satisfaction – meaning that he often goaded people into challenging him, then had them arrested for the illegal practice of duelling. His own duels were pardoned by the King.

He was a patron of the poet Dryden who described him as: "A lecherous chemist, fiddler, statesman and buffoon," who, "laughed himself from court, then sought relief by forming parties, but could ne'er be chief." He was also: "A man so various that he seemed to be, not one, but all mankind's epitome."

He was also known as a wit, adulterer and bully, a ridiculer and puncturer of ambitions, and a braggart, but he remained loyal to the King above all else. Others claimed he didn't know the meaning of loyalty, and he was accused of having the King's horoscope, "treasonably drawn up."

At the death of Charles, Buckingham retired to Yorkshire, and followed his pursuits of hunting and alchemy, more assiduously. In the last ten years of his life he suffered from failing heath. He was in debt, and he did not get on with James II, who failed to convert him to Catholicism. In 1686 he was said to be, "worn to a thread with whoring."

In April of the following year, he caught a chill while out hunting. He was taken to the house of a tenant of his at Kirby Moorside, which still remains as a farmhouse today. There, although he begged to be taken to his house in York, he fell into a coma, and died. Once the foremost man in the kingdom, after the King, all his power and all his riches were nothing to him now.

So badly was he in debt that his widow, the Duchess, who survived him by seventeen years, was left nothing. His estate was vested in trustees to pay off what he owed, and she survived on what she inherited from her father, Lord Fairfax. Buckingham had no legitimate son, and his title died with him.

Why had, "the most accomplished man of the age," and once the wealthiest man in England, died a virtual pauper? At one time, while handling foreign policy for Charles, he had received massive bribes from the King of France, then the richest monarch in Europe. Where had all the money gone?

Ostentatious living might be thought to be the reason, but although very rich, Buckingham had always been careful. While in exile in Paris he retained just two servants – although he was better off at the time than Charles, who kept scores about him.

A close retainer of his latter years, Brian Fairfax, revealed one reason. The Duke's experiments in alchemy, "were one of his greatest expenses." A by-product of these had been the creation of a glass factory at Lambeth, needed to make his chemical retorts.

An eminent historian of the time, Bishop Burnet, recorded that Buck-ingham dabbled in chemistry, "and for some years thought he was very near to finding the philosopher's stone."

All his life Buckingham had been living in the shadow of his great father, who had ruled the country through puppet kings – first James I, next Charles I. The second Duke wanted to emulate his parent, and he brought an inventive mind to the task. First, he sought to influence the young Charles II through their boyhood association. Then he introduced him to Thomas Hobbes, finally he embroiled him in the licentious vices of the age – and finding in this Charles' greatest weakness, he paraded before him a series of mistresses, including the notorious Lady Castle-maine, Buckingham's cousin, whom Charles preferred above his Queen, and sought through these women to manipulate his monarch. The fact that he ultimately failed reflected more on his unfitness for high office, than his assiduousness in acquiring it. "He wanted power for power's sake, and had no talent for using it," was the verdict of his contemporaries – his scandalous and arrogant lifestyle brought about his downfall. Perhaps his interest in alchemy ran along similar lines.

Alchemy – the forerunner of modern chemistry, involved magical practices, astrology, and chemical experiments with various substances. The object of this was the search for the philosopher's stone – a transmuting agent of great power. The stone, which Buckingham belie-ved himself so close to discovering, was said to be a universal remedy for human ills and diseases, known as, "the elixir of life, or grand elixir," a universal panacea, which could restore youth, and prolong life.

Entering Europe via Spain, in the 12th century, the knowledge was said to be the repository of wisdom of the ancient Egyptians, carried to Spain by the Islamic invasions.

The stone is found, "through the conjunction of masculine and feminine principles." According to alchemical tradition, the searcher must, "visit the inward parts of earth; by rectifying, thou shalt find the hidden stone."

What had the richest man of his age found, in his secret experiments in York and in what way were they dependant on young women? Had he spent so much money on his research that he had finally discovered the stone he sought, and if so, what was it? What black arts did he dabble in at York?

Difficult questions to answer, but perhaps they throw some light on why the Duke was so anxious to return to his house in York after he fell ill, and when he was dying. And perhaps, after all, Buckingham had the last laugh on the contemporaries who dubbed him, "the lecherous chemist."

He was buried in Westminster Abbey, close by his friend and monarch, Charles II, but although his body lies in London, something of his extraordinary personality seems to linger in York.

It was some years after I met Mrs Stanley at the Cock and Bottle, that I learned the Stanleys had left York. Mrs Stanley, it seems, had died, while still a young woman. She had certainly betrayed no signs of ill-health when I had seen her last.

New landlords have the Cock and Bottle, and the restless changing sea of faces moves ever on, as generation merges with generation.

But there is a stone, with a face that never changes, except to appear – and disappear . . .

Landlady Brenda Stanley points out the area of a wall where a face appears in certain lighting conditions with the likeness of a Cavalier.

4

MURDER AT
THE MANOR

This story is about a young man, the youngest of eleven children, and his father's favourite. He was bequeathed the lease of a good-sized farm at Bramhall in Cheshire, of which he was master at the relatively early age of twenty four. He was a handsome young man, a genteel dresser, and in addition to the good fortune of inheriting the farm, over the heads of his elder siblings, he had much success with the ladies of the neighbourhood – so much, in fact, that it led to his downfall.

On an early Spring day in 1823, at Chester Assizes, he was the subject of an address by the Attorney General.

"My Lord, and gentlemen of the jury. The prisoner at the bar has been charged with the wilful murder of Betty Shallcross. In this case it will not be necessary that I should call your attention to the law of murder. If, by the evidence adduced, the charge is brought home to the prisoner, it is a crime of such enormity that you will not hesitate in finding him guilty. Cases of murder, gentlemen, are seldom, if ever, committed in the face of day or in the presence of any witness, and must therefore, depend on circumstantial evidence, and when this evidence is connected and none of the links broken, then there is no evidence so strong. I shall then, without further comment, call your attention to the evidence brought before you, which it will require you most minutely to examine as the charge depends on various minute facts, such as the contradictory accounts which the prisoner has given of himself, and of other facts, connected with the case."

"Gentlemen of the jury, it will appear by the evidence brought before you that the prisoner and the deceased had been on terms of intimacy for a considerable time, and that she, at the time of her death, was far advanced in pregnancy by him; it will also appear that another young woman, of the name of Mary Coups, was pregnant by the prisoner, and that he had promised marriage to her; but deferred it under pretence that his uncle was averse to the match. Gentlemen, the prisoner, Samuel Fallows, is a farmer and resides in Bramhall, and the deceased Betty Shallcross, lived with Mr R C Morrey at Woodley, a distance of six miles from the residence of the prisoner."

"The prisoner was in the habit of usually attending Stockport market, and on the 21st March last, it will be proved that the deceased went to Miss Leigh, desiring her to carry a letter directed to the prisoner, and to leave it at Mr Hickman's, the sign of the Plough, in Stockport. Gentlemen, the letter was delivered, as will be proved in evidence, by Mrs Hickman to the prisoner, who received it, and being asked by her if there would be any answer, replied that there would be none, but that she had given him the letter. After having received the letter, the prisoner returned home from Stockport, about 5 o'clock in the afternoon, and assisted his servant to milk the cows. It must be recollected gentlemen, that when the prisoner went to market on the morning of the 21st, he was dressed in a black coat, cord breeches, and light coloured gaiters or leggings; and it will be proved to you, that, after assisting his servant in milking, he was seen on the road from Stockport, which is the direct road to Woodley, and that the prisoner did not return home that evening."

"The following morning, which was a Saturday, about 10 o'clock, the body of the deceased was found in an outbuilding, belonging to Mr Morrey, in such a mangled state as required more nerve than, I think, anyone present possesses to approach, and which will also show the violent struggling the deceased had used to avoid her fate."

"Gentlemen, her throat was most dreadfully cut, and near her lay a razor, undoubtedly the fatal instrument which had caused her death. Suspicion immediately fell on the prisoner. He was apprehended and questioned as to where he had been on that night. He said he went to see Mary Coups, but being wet through, had returned home from Mobberley. (The learned gentleman here stated the principle features of the two sworn statements of the prisoner, made to the Deputy Constable, and before the Inquest.)

"A witness, gentlemen, will be called before you, who will prove having seen him under the Croft Bridge, between six and seven o'clock on the following morning, near his own house, and that when this witness came up to him, he ran off in a contrary direction to his own dwelling."

"With this chain of evidence gentlemen, I shall call your attention, and show to you that both his declarations are false; that he was at Stockport, at seven o'clock in the evening, on his way to Woodley, undoubtedly prepared to accomplish his diabolical purpose. If innocent, it will be for him to prove where he was on the whole of that night, and more particularly, what became of his clothes. There is another material point to which I beg to draw your attention – a razor, covered with blood, was found within a yard and a half of the body of the deceased – it was an old razor, loose in one of the rivets, and similar to one which has been frequently used by a man, lately in the service of the prisoner. Having stated thus much, and which I am prepared to substantiate, from unquestionable testimony, I shall leave it with you to say, whether the prisoner be innocent or guilty of this murder." With a flourish, the A G concluded his address.

Subsequent evidence showed that the local squire, Captain Humphreys of Bramall Hall, had Fallows taken into custody on a charge of bastardy – then an offence – on Mary Coups. Humphreys had remonstrated with Fallows on the cruelty of jilting the girl, after the banns had been read in church. As a magistrate, Humphreys kept him in custody, until he agreed to marry the girl, on condition of being released. On his release Fallows again changed his mind, and refused to marry her. This took place in January of the same year. Fallows also gave two different and unsubstantiated accounts of where he was on the night of the murder, which tended to suggest that he was a man of uncertain temperament, even if he wasn't simply lying.

His first account claimed that he had intended to walk a distance of thirteen miles to see Mary Coups, but that he turned back, drenched by rain, and arriving home late, and not wanting to disturb the household, hung his wet clothes on a hedge to dry and went to sleep in a hay-loft. The clothes could not be found later, and he suggested that they must have been stolen.

The second account he gave, claimed he had spent the night waiting in the fields for poachers, and that he had returned wet through, and left his clothes to dry on the hedge, and they had disappeared. He said he told the first story because he had been told, "people would come against him and say anything." He wished to catch the poachers because he had been accused of taking hares by the people at Bramall Hall – an allegation they denied when asked about it.

But the main piece of evidence against him concerned the razor found near the body of the victim. Witnesses denied that it belonged to Woodley Manor, where the murder had been committed, but a servant of Fallows thought he recognised it as one he had used while sharing a room with his master.

Ralph Saxton of Manor Farm Cottage, Woodley, was the person who, with Mary Tweedale, found Betty Shallcross on the Saturday morning, and the razor, about a yard and a half from where she lay. In evidence he stated that it had a little bit of the horn handle loose or broken, and this was cited as an identifying feature, which marked the razor as one thought to belong to Fallows – yet no similar razors were said to exist either at Manor Farm Cottage or the Manor House itself.

Woodley Manor was a relatively recent creation of a family named Cheetham Morrey. Wealthy colliery owners, they bought Manor Farm Cottage, which was a much older building, its farmland, and built a large house which they named Woodley Manor.

Betty Shallcross was a servant here, and other servants remembered Samuel Fallows calling on her in the months leading up to the murder, the two having originally met at Stockport market. Betty had apparently told her mistress, at the manor, that she would be leaving their service by the end of March, and she allegedly told a neighbour that she was to be married secretly at Manchester Registry Office, and that Fallows had told her not to tell anyone.

Evidence revealed that no-one had actually seen Fallows at Woodley on the night of the murder, but there were two eye-witness accounts which conflicted with his story of where he had been. Daniel Clarke, an acquaintance, thought he saw Fallows at seven in the evening going down Millgate from Stockport Market. It was implied that this is the route to Woodley, but in fact, it is a short town-centre street, with branches in various directions. It is also usually fairly crowded on market days, even to the present time, thus increasing the chances of mistaken identity – since the witness did not speak to the person he took to be Fallows, but saw him from a distance.

The other witness was a boy of ten, John Minshull, who lived near to Fallows in Bramhall. He said that he saw Fallows at seven on Saturday morning, coming under Croft Bridge from the direction of Stockport, and observed him wearing a black coat and light coloured breeches from a distance of twenty yards in good light. Fallows changed direction and headed off away from his own house. Croft bridge is not far from

Fallows' farm, and the change of direction was not conclusive evidence of guilt – if he were searching for traps – but it was taken to be. The boy did not say that he noticed any bloodstains on Fallows' clothing, but the whole point of the missing breeches and leggings was the suggestion that they had been disposed of to conceal the fact that they were drenched with blood.

The only evidence, other than circumstantial, which tied Fallows into the murder was the razor, which was found in a shippon, near the body, by Ralph Saxton, the farmer at Manor Farm Cottage, who had the use of the shippon, which was owned by the Cheetham Morreys.

The most curious feature of this evidence, which was not challenged by the defence – in fact the defence seems to have acted very poorly on behalf of Fallows – was that the razor was singular by virtue of a loose rivet, and a broken or loose horn handle. How many razors of this period, of similar construction, developed a similar fault? A good defence lawyer could have quickly collected several in a similar condition, to scotch the theory of its uniqueness. It is even more curious that in large farming households, with servants and labourers, such as the Manor, and Manor Farm Cottage, no similar example of an ageing razor could be found. Also, during the course of her long distance courtship with Fallows, whom she saw infrequently, had Betty Shallcross no admirers, open, or secret, among the men of the immediate neighbourhood, if not the same, or adjacent household?

The tight alibis of Woodley Manor, and Manor Farm Cottage, raise a whisper of suspicion in the mind. The ingenuous confessions of Fallows' servants as to his whereabouts, and the ownership of the razor, or one like it, seems to indicate a household taken by surprise, or even a desire to incriminate the young man, who had inherited a farm ahead of his peers, and then scandalised the neighbourhood with his cavalier adventures among women. Two households – one determined that the hand of guilt should not fall on them, despite the body being on their premises, and the other, miles away in Bramhall, surprised and frightened – anxious to unload the burden of guilt. One can almost hear then saying: "Oh, you've gone too far this time Sam!" The case for the defence, ironically enough, seemed to rest on character witnesses. Various neighbours in Bramhall, even the magistrate from Bramall Hall, Captain Humphreys, all testified to, "the previous good character" of Fallows.

The trial, on the 11th of April, 1823, had taken from nine in the morning to half past four in the afternoon. The jury had heard the

APPENDIX.

Particulars of the Conduct,

Previous to and at the time of Execution,

OF

SAMUEL FALLOWS,

On *Monday*, *April* 14th, 1823.

The sun of Monday morning was th
arose on the earthly career of Samuel Fallow
been arranged, that according to the plan ad
two last county executions, the malefactor sho
veyed early in the morning from the castle to
instead of being dragged through the city
amidst an immense concourse of people at a
just before they were to be launched into ete
the best authority we learn that on Sunday
retained that firm and undaunted appearance
before had occasion to notice in him. He stri
to rest soon after ten, and the person who ha
attended him, assured us that he appeared to
composure. About four o'clock he arose au
self; and presently after, his brother and
mitted to an interview with him. One of th
the culprit asked was, whether they had l
old clothes; they replied in the affirmative.
a bowl of coffee at Mr Dunstan's, at five
taken on foot out of the Debtor's door in th
escorted by the under-sheriff and officers
where he was delivered to the city sheriffs,
tendance with a cart, to carry him to the ci
this walk, he trod with a firm step, and
the least symptom of weakness. Mounte
in the cart, he was thus conveyed to his
and, although it was so early in the mo
course of people had assembled to witnes
cession, which proceeded through the
the castle, along Nicholas-street and
the city gaol. The chaplain attended hi
notwithstanding the most pressing solici
ties, Fallows declined making any co
every reason to believe that this proce

REPORT

OF THE

Trial of Samuel Fallows,

Charged with the

MURDER

OF

BETTY SHALLCROSS SINGLE WOMAN,

AT WOODLEY,

In the Township of Bredbury,

At CHESTER SPRING ASSIZES, April 11th, 1823,

BEFORE THE

HON. C. WARREN, AND THE HON. S. MARSHALL,

His Majesty's Justices,

And the following Jury:—

JOHN BAXTER, FOREMAN.	JOSEPH COLLIER.
JOHN KIRKHAM.	JOHN HUTCHINSON.
THOMAS COOK.	JOHN LANDOR.
SAMUEL NORBURY.	THOMAS WARD.
JOHN ALCOCK.	JOHN BRACEGIRDLE.
SAMUEL BULL.	THOMAS BRAY.

Counsel for the Prosecution,

Mr HILL, (Attorney-General,) and Mr ASHWORTH.

Counsel for the Prisoner,

Mr SERJEANT CROSS, and Mr WILLIAMS.

Stockport:

PRINTED BY J. LOMAX, ADVERTISER OFFICE.

*A local pamphlet described
the trial and execution*

evidence of the surgeon who examined the dead body of the murder victim, which witnesses stated had been discovered face down, the cap knocked off, and her apron flung up over her shoulder. The surgeon, John Cheetham, said he found wounds on the top and back of the head inflicted by a blunt instrument. A five inch long gash in the throat, on the left side, and continuing over the collar bone, had severed the jugular vein, and was probably inflicted by the razor. Two contusions on the back of the left hand, from a blunt instrument, had probably been received as she tried to protect her head. There was also a severe bruise on the left cheek, near the mouth, and a deep cut to the bone, on the right thumb, two inches long, and probably sustained from the razor, while trying to protect her throat.

The jury retired for only a few minutes before they were back with their verdict. In the interval, Samuel Fallows was allowed to sit down on a bench, and ate two oranges and a biscuit, "with perfect sang froid," as the correspondent of the Stockport Advertiser noted – although more likely it was due to exhaustion after standing all day. He was a fair-complexioned young man, about 5ft 10ins tall, wearing a smart blue suit, black waistcoat, and a black neckerchief, according to the same correspondent. During the course of the trial he had maintained an unrevealing composure.

The jury returned to court and the foreman pronounced the verdict – guilty!

The clerk of the court informed Fallows that he had pleaded not guilty, putting himself upon God and his country, which country had found him guilty, and called upon him to say why sentence of death should not be passed upon him. Fallows did not reply, but burst into tears.

The Chief Justice then made some sanctimonious comments about Fallows being only hours from the presence of, "that Being who searches the hearts of the children of man," and the need for sincere contrition and humble repentance. He then pronounced sentence in the usual way with the addition that: "On Monday next you are to be taken to the place of execution, for a second sun shall not rise and set upon you, and you are then to be hanged by the neck until you are dead, and your body afterwards given to the surgeons for dissection."

Quick justice indeed, and perhaps even deserving justice for the heartless person who brutally battered and slashed a comely young woman, in the prime of life, who was also an expectant mother.

But was Samuel that person? There is little likelihood of his being convicted on the same evidence nowadays – which is why the Attorney General in presenting the case for the prosecution made the ludicrous assertion that murder is seldom, if ever, committed before witnesses, and that conviction always depended on circumstantial evidence. He was relying on the ignorance of the jury, whose lack of knowledge of criminal procedures would have been much greater, in 1823, than any equivalent modern jury, who will all have seen trials on television. Modern forensic evidence may well have been able to establish Fallows innocence – or his guilt.

Samuel Fallows, himself, believed that the evidence would be insufficient to convict him. Urged repeatedly by the chaplain, and governor of the city jail, to confess, and relieve his conscience, he refused to do so. He was reluctant to attend divine service on Sunday morning, the day before he was due to be executed, and made some excuse in the afternoon, presumably having heard enough about heaven and hell in the morning.

The anxiousness with which he was enjoined to confess seems to have reflected more on the conscience of those who had determined his guilt. The Advertiser correspondent became quite petulant about it:

"It is exceedingly to be regretted that this false pride of his, should have so far prevailed over the young man, as to prevent him unbosoming his conscience, and thus obstructing the way to a throne of mercy. The evidence upon the trial, which we have given at length, is such as to assure the most scrupulous mind of the correctness of the verdict; but still, for the sake of the unhappy criminal, it is desirable that he should have made a direct confession."

The untidy fact remained that he didn't confess. He seems to have been told to remain silent by his brother and sister, who brought his clothes to the jail. The most that he would say was that he had, "confessed to God." For this he was described by the correspondent as possessed of an, "unusual portion of pride, obstinacy, and obduracy."

On the Monday morning he was taken from Chester Castle to the city jail by the under-sheriffs. There he stripped, and put on fresh underwear, "without any apparent concern", according to an eyewitness. For his breakfast, he drank three cups of coffee, and ate some bread and butter. The time had now come for him to mount the scaffold, and he permitted a clergyman to give him the bread and wine of the holy sacrament, after which he ascended the platform with agility, and a firm and unwavering step.

According to *The Advertiser*: "Those who had the nearest and steadiest view of him, affirm, that during the awful process of fastening and adjusting the rope, there were not the slightest marks of trepidation observable about him. He was not above three minutes outside the jail, during which the chaplain in vain pressed the necessity and advantage of confession. He seemed to pay no regard to the surrounding multitude, and did not appear even to look at them. At one o'clock, every preparation being made, the drop fell, and the poor unfortunate man was launched into a world of spirits. He struggled hard for two or three minutes. Then the body of the young fellow was ordered to be given to the surgeons of the infirmary."

This and much more sanctimonious claptrap was published, having been previously advertised by the local paper as, "particulars of the conduct previous to, and at the time of execution of Samuel Fallows." No doubt they were sold out.

So who was guilty in the case of Samuel Fallows? In the first place, the murderer of Betty Shallcross, supposing this was not Fallows. If it was not Fallows, then the guilty party for the judicial murder of the young man was Society – arraigned, indicted, and in the dock. Since a noose won't fit round that many necks, and the culprits are all dead, the best we can do is try to ensure a modern judicial system can't make the same mistakes. We do, however, still use juries of ordinary men and women, untrained in sifting complicated facts, and lawyers still use the same old tricks of smear and implication.

Of course, Fallows may have been guilty. If not, he was extremely unlucky to have been out alone on the night in question, without an adequate alibi, to have been seen in contradictory places by two people, and to have lost his clothes, when they were needed as material evidence.

We shall never know the absolute truth, but there has been a curious sequel in recent years. Woodley Manor no longer exists, all that remains of the place is the yard of a haulage company. Samuel Fallows' farm has long since gone, swallowed up by suburban housing estates of the South Manchester commuter belt. But, by chance, Manor Farm Cottage, in Woodley, remains, and the shippon, where the body of Betty Shallcross was found in a pool of blood, was demolished only in the seventies, after becoming unsafe.

A light was seen moving about in the blocked-off upper storey of Woodley Manor Farm Cottages.

A recent occupier of Manor Farm Cottage, Mrs Pauline Lambie, has a curious tale to tell. Not long after she and her husband, Ian, moved into the cottage they noticed that quite frequently, they could hear someone on the stairs. Footsteps would sound when they knew no-one was there, and no-one ever appeared. Then, one night, some little boys knocked on the door, to tell them that they had seen someone walking back and forth, with a candle, in an upstairs room. The room in question was right at the top of the house, which is an old three-storeyed stone building, with mullioned windows. There are two windows, facing the road, in this room, and the light had moved from one to the other, as if someone were pacing back and forth. This gave the Lambies a shock, because they knew that the room was sealed off from the rest of the house, and definitely unoccupied. The only entry to it was through their own quarters, and the upper floor had been sealed off with hardboard as a loft, because the refurbishment of the old property was not complete at that time. Investigation showed that no-one had disturbed the hardboard, and no-one could be up there without the Lambies' knowledge. Having heard about the murder by then, the couple were no longer surprised to hear that a woman in a long dress had also been seen one night, jumping the stream in front of the cottage, and walking up a path in the garden which is no longer there, and hasn't been for many years.

But although the Lambies' knew a murder had taken place, they did not, at the time, know the exact details, and were under the impression it had occurred at the cottage where they lived.

When they first went to live in the cottage the old shippon was still standing, and was used for stabling horses. Entirely innocent of its history they were surprised when a young girl, who stabled her horse there, complained that she always felt uneasy in the place. The girl said that she didn't like to be in the stable, because she always felt as if someone were watching her, and the horse seemed upset and restless while stabled, and was always glad to get away.

"Don't worry," Mrs Lambie told her, "the murder took place in the farmhouse." Of course, she was wrong, and did not find out until some years after the shippon had been demolished, that it was the actual site of the murder.

So whose restless spirit seems to manifest itself at Manor Farm Cottage? If it were Samuel Fallows, why is he heard inside the cottage, where he never had occasion to set foot in life? His visits to Woodley ended at the Manor House, according to witnesses. And if he met Betty Shallcross in the shippon, so close to the cottage, why was he not disturbed, or seen by someone, on a busy farm? Is the woman in the long dress, seen skipping across the stream, a shade of Betty Shallcross, or perhaps Mary Tweedale, who found Betty's body in the shippon, and calmly examined all the blackened and blood-clotted wounds, which she recounted in detail at the trial? And what of Ralph Saxton, the farmer at Manor Farm Cottage, who found the razor which connected Fallows to the murder – is it he who walks distractedly back and forth with a candle in the top room? And why did Fallows relatives want him to keep quiet – did he, or they, know something which could have incriminated others?

Unless ghosts talk, we shall never know.

5

ROMANS WHO WENT "BUMP, BUMP, BUMP" IN THE NIGHT

"Time warps are not beyond the imagination of men. But 'imagination' being the key word, this is where they stay, relegated to the realms of science fiction, and not seriously considered to have any direct bearing on human life. Yet this is despite Einstein's theory of the manipulation of time by physical means, like speed, or gravity. According to current scientific theory the moon walkers aged a fraction less than their contemporaries – because when you travel very fast, time slows down. At the speed of light, time stops, and beyond it a regression into the past occurs."

I once wrote this in relation to what must be the most curious, known, extant haunting, in Britain today. At the time, I considered that "time" might in some way explain, or help to explain, the phenomena, and we conducted a series of experiments, to try to verify this. However, since time and space are inextricably linked, and the earth is now several billion miles further on, in its orbit of the sun, which in turn, continues to move through the galaxy, the "space of time" between the ever present "now", and the original occurrence of the phenomena, seems, to me, to be an un-bridgable gap. The time warp theory seemed neat, but what is a "time warp"? Let the physicist explain.

Treasurer's House is a nicely-proportioned town mansion, lying within the shadow of York Minster. With rolling Dutch gables, a warm red pantiled roof, and walls of large white limestone blocks, it is one of the ancient city's most attractive settings. To the front, its leaded windows look out onto a lovely formal garden, with lawns, paths, fish-pond and fountain, all enclosed within a protective mellow brick wall, shaded by mature trees. On a clear night, one may see clear across the galaxy as a young astronomer, John Goodricke did, when he discovered the pulsating stars, Cephei, Lyrae and Algol from an upper window in Treasurer's House. Had he not been looking at the heavens, he might have discovered something equally interesting nearby. In the cellars, to be exact. One hesitates in describing the unusual phenomena associated with Treasurer's House – they are so many and varied that it is probably safer to continue with the history of the building.

Above ground, the garden of Treasurer's House, sun-dappled, with a delightful array of Greco-Roman statues.

The oldest parts of the house date back to the 17th century, although it is possible some of the cellars may be medieval. There has been some sort of building on the spot right back to Roman times. Heavily restored by a wealthy Yorkshire manufacturer, Mr Frank Green, in this century, it was given by him to the National Trust, who have opened it to the public. Although it is possible to walk round most parts of the house, the most inaccessible cellars are out of bounds – mainly because they are approached down low, arched, back-breaking, and frequently waterlogged passageways. In one of these cellars Harry Martindale, a level-headed

York policeman, saw a troop of Roman soldiers walk out of one solid wall, and disappear through another, despite looking as real and substantial as you or I.

From the charming courtyard at the rear of Treasurer's House, with its ancient cobbling, and avenue of plane trees, one may observe the external windows of a semi-basement room, now used as an office. It is from this room, that a number of people have entered another dimension of experience. In the narrow cobbled alleyway known as Chapterhouse Street, which runs along the side of the mansion, you can see a window grating at pavement level. About nine or ten feet below this, inside the cellar which it serves, one is something like a foot or so above the original Roman road level. And here, hidden by a blank wall, and buried by tons of earth and debris, lies a mystery, which, one day, someone may unravel.

It is a mystery which has brought journalists from all parts of the world, and even resulted in the invitation, extended by a Dutch television company, to two witches, to see what they could "pick-up" in the cellar. What they did pick up was interesting, but not Roman. Which is not surprising, considering all the other ages which are represented there. Among the many ghosts said to haunt the place is that of George Aislaby, killed in a duel with a friend of our old friend, the Duke of Buckingham. The story is that Aislaby's sister-in-law stayed out all night after attending a ball at the Duke of Buckingham's house in Skeldergate. She was with her fiance, Jonathan Jennings, and Aislaby; no doubt considering the reputation of the Duke's friends; felt that honour had been besmirched. Rather unwisely, he agreed to redeem it through the medium of a duel.

The Duke was a good swordsman, and so, unfortunately, was his friend Jonathan Jennings. George Aislaby, redeemed his family's honour, but it cost him his life. He was carried mortally wounded back to Treasurer's House, where he died. Jennings, fearing the consequences of the law, borrowed a coach from his friend, the Duke, and made haste for London, to beg a pardon of Charles II. He eventually returned to York, a free man, but his former fiancee would have nothing to do with him, or any other man, and died a spinster.

According to York historian, John Mitchell, an interesting link with this story was given him by a man who said that whenever he passed the door of Treasurer's House, in Chapterhouse Street, as he frequently did, he felt, "an acute sense that he must protect himself from some violent attack." The feeling was even more pronounced when he was walking with anyone else. But he knew nothing of the Aislaby story.

I have twice heard similar comments about the same proximity, completely spontaneously from people without foreknowledge of either story. The first came from a friend of mine, an antiquary, with a fine, appreciative sense of music, and old buildings. He remarked, as we were sitting in the garden of Treasurer's House, not far from the door into the garden near Chapterhouse Street, that he felt, "the atmosphere" was antagonistic towards him, and he attributed it in some curious way to a "racial" source, which he said made him feel ill at ease, and that he felt it strongly only in this spot. He is by racial admixture a Hibernian Celt.

The second was evoked in my wife, Jean, as we approached the door on Chapterhouse Street, when I was taking her to look round the mansion for the first time. She commented that it was the sort of place one could expect to be attacked in. When I told her of the other stories, she seemed surprised, and said that it must be something to do with the narrowness of the street, which made it likely that strangers would have to pass by one another closely.

Inside Treasurer's House, upstairs, in the North East corner of the building, is the Tapestry Room. Possibly the most atmospheric room in the mansion, it is redolent of the 17th century, and that is the age of the blackened wooden panelling, which covers the walls, the Cromwellian, Civil War armour, and the table and chairs. Dark and silent, with a slightly uneven bare wooden floor, the result of age and the primitive adze, used to shape the boards, it is said always to feel much colder that the rest of the building. Personally I find it interesting and pleasant, and have never noticed unusual cold. But the story goes that a wife murdered her husband here, when he threatened to introduce his mistress into the house. Who, or when, I don't know.

The other upstairs rooms are more disturbing to my taste. In the main bedrooms the beds all seem somehow badly orientated, and the fireplaces are in walls where I would not expect them to be situated. One bedroom has an excessively miserable, dark, reddish wall decoration, and if any room were haunted that ought to be, but, apparently, it isn't. It is called the King's room, and is said to have been slept in by royal visitors.

Treasurer's House is so called because it used to be the house of the Treasurer to York Minster, which, in the Middle Ages, was a great and wealthy ecclesiastical institution, with land, farms, tithes, and lots of rent coming in. The Treasurer was therefore a very important person in medieval York, and rated a big house from which to conduct his business. The spot was probably always associated with the Church, even before there was a mansion there. The Dutch witches "picked up" on an unidentified wretch who seemed to be in some sort of ecclesiastic prison. He was in deadly fear of his life, because, from what they could make out, there was some dreadful conflagration going on at the time, in which most of York seemed to be burning, and of course, poor, whoever-he-was had been forgotten. This interested the National Trust's Administrator who did some research, and discovered that there WAS such a thing as an ecclesiastical prison, behind the Minister somewhere in that area, in medieval times, and that the fire was very likely the great fire of York.

It's only fair to say of the witches that they hadn't been told about the Romans, so it wasn't surprising they didn't mention them. But even if they knew about the fire of York, it seems doubtful that they would know about Church prisons, or that one existed nearby.

With this amazing psychic track record, it isn't surprising that Treasurer's House has won a place in the Guinness Book of Records – for having the oldest known ghosts in England, that is, the Romans, seen by Harry Martindale, and others.

When I descended into the cellars with Harry for the first time, to hear the story from his own lips, I was quite open-minded, but determined to question him on the authentic points of the haunting. As we stooped down the long and tortuous passageways, leading to the cellar, Harry pointed out a Roman column base, set back in a wall recess, which had been discovered about eight feet below the present road level, above it, in the street outside. He explained that a similar base had also been recently found, when the road outside had been excavated. He had been working in the haunted cellar, as a young apprentice plumber, installing central heating pipes, where archaeologists had recently been digging on the very spot where he stood his ladder! "I didn't know it at the time, but I was on the site of a Roman road. The archaeologists had excavated part of the cellar to about 18 inches depth, which reached the original Roman road level," he explained.

Harry was a big-framed police constable, approaching middle age, when we entered the cellars to re-live his experiences of twenty years before. He told me that after 18 years in the police, he had never experienced anything quite so frightening as what happened on that cold February day in the early 1950's, probably about 1953, but he couldn't be certain of the date, although he was certain of the experience. "I had worked a full day already, and came back on the second day. I knew that the place was old, but not that old – I'd put my ladder on a Roman road!" Harry mounted the ladder and began his work on the wall of the cellar. As he worked, a musical note intruded on his consciousness – it sounded like a bugle. "I thought it was a wireless, and wondered how I could hear it down there." Next moment Harry got the shock of his life, as an apparently solid object came through the wall at the side of his ladder.

Like most people, he reacted instinctively – falling, rather than jumping, from the ladder. He scrambled to the far side of the cellar, which isn't very big, and watched in terrified amazement as the short figure of a man advanced into the room – between Harry and the exit.

A series of low, vaulted passageways lead into the haunted cellar where Steve Cliffe and Tom Anderson examine the Roman road level.

"It had passed within inches of me, and I just couldn't fathom what it could be. I wanted to get as far away as possible. In 18 years in the police my hair has never stood on end, but it bristled then."

The short swarthy figure was wearing sandals cross-gartered to the knee, a kilt of plain sack-like material, dyed in an uneven green colour, while at its right side, facing Harry, was a short sword, hanging in a scabbard, and on its head was a highly polished helmet, with a plume of long birds' feathers. As the weary-looking figure trudged into the centre

A Roman column base excavated in one of the passageways – one of several to have been discovered lining the Roman military way to the headquarters building.

of the cellar, Harry realised with a shock that the bottom part of its legs were only visible as it passed over the excavated portion of the cellar – at the original level of the Roman road!

Artist's impression of the Roman ghost scene. (Martin Mills)

It was immediately followed by a soldier on a horse – "like a great big cart-horse, with hairy, bushy legs," according to Harry. The rider carried a round shield with a raised metal boss in the centre. After the horse and rider came men in pairs, almost stumbling along, looking very tired, mud-splattered, and dispirited. Harry could see their burnished helmets reflecting in the bright light of his inspection lamps, and the different coloured plumes of feathers – from colourful birds, seemed to fill the small cellar. Between 20 or a dozen men filed through the cellar, diagonally across the dip in the floor, where even the horse's hairy hooves came into view. One carried a much-used horn, short and straight, like a modern hunting horn, and dented at the wide end, which Harry was to hear blown again, as the man disappeared through the opposite wall.

Harry Martindale describes his experience in the haunted Roman cellar. The Roman road level is immediately in front of the group.
(Photo: Huddersfield Daily Examiner)

"I thought they would see me. They looked as real as normal people – I even heard the horse, and a kind of murmuring coming from the centre of the room, and a muffled tread. They were small men – the only Romans I'd seen were big blokes in films – and they looked as if they would have to shave twice a day, with dark skin, not black like negroes, but darker than we are, more like continentals."

All the men wore similar green skirts, or kilts, above the knee, and leather sandals, thonged up their legs. They also carried short swords at their right hips. Harry thinks he may have seen spears, but is not certain about this. In fact, his anxiousness to stick to the facts of what he saw, and not be coerced by suggestion, is a remarkable feature of his subsequent interview with a Roman expert.

At the time, however, he was not worrying about details of Roman military costume, but how to get out of the cellar alive, or at least sane. After the apparently solid troop of soldiers had filed across, and through the opposite wall, without once looking in his direction, Harry rushed to get out. As he went, he heard the horn blown again, and the sound of their muffled tread fading away.

The long passages out of the cellar seemed interminable, but at last Harry staggered out into the light of day, bumping straight into the curator of Treasurer's House, who took one look at him and said: "You've seen the Romans, haven't you?" The relief which Harry felt then, defies description, as he realised that other people had known the same awful experience, and that he wasn't insane, after all.

The curator produced a book, which contained at least two other written eyewitness accounts of the phenomena, and told Harry to write down what he had seen, in it, while it was still fresh in his memory. This is probably the reason why he remembers the details so well, and although the curator is dead, and the book missing, at least some record of it remains. According to Harry, one of these witnesses was an American, who, operating on the theory that the haunting recurred every seven years, sat waiting on the appointed day, and saw them.

"I still can't understand how the past can impose on the present here, and why I was chosen," said Harry. He had no interest in either ghosts, or Romans, said he was not in the least bit psychic, and insisted that the experience was totally distasteful, and one he hoped never to repeat. For many years he was very careful about repeating the story to anyone, but eventually decided that it didn't matter whether people believed him or not.

At the time, Harry knew of only one other person who had seen the Romans, while working at Treasurer's House, after his own sighting. This man, who was ill in hospital, didn't want to discuss the subject with anyone. Since then, a lady has come forward with a similar experience to relate.

Harry was a convinced Christian, at the time of my interview with him in the haunted cellar, and he rejected my suggestion that a medium or clairvoyant might throw light on the matter of the ghosts. "As a Christian I'm not interested in witches and mediums," he said.

The description of the Roman accoutrements Harry gave the Roman expert, who questioned him, dated the apparitions as Roman auxiliary troops of about 390AD – a time when the Roman Empire was collapsing under a barbarian onslaught. Harry had no way of knowing beforehand

Harry Martindale: He refused to speak of his experience for 20 years.

that Romans, unlike most soldiers, always wore their swords on the right, instead of the left hip. This, and other details, convinced the experts of a degree of authenticity in the sighting described by Harry, which they could not explain.

I have heard the tape of this interview, and frequently, when led astray in the course of it, Harry replied saying: "If I said that, I'd be guessing, and I don't want to guess. I've never looked at a book on Romans, and if I don't remember a detail, I don't want to guess." He ended with a question. "Do they come once, or twice, or three times a day, whether there's anyone there or not?"

John Mitchell, the York historian, described a previous Roman sighting at the house during a fancy dress ball. A lady guest wandered into the basement during a game of hide and seek. Seeing what she took to be another guest in fancy dress, by a passageway, she approached, but was surprised when he sternly held up his spear to bar her path. Annoyed and flustered, she returned to the host to ask him who the rude man, dressed as a Roman, was. The reply was that no-one had arrived in anything remotely resembling such a disguise!

Another sighting occurred round about the time of Harry's, but probably before it, in the early fifties. It was in either November, January, or February, according to the female witness, who didn't want her identity disclosed. It happened on a very cold day, in the late afternoon, or early evening, because the witness, who was the wife of the then caretaker at Treasurer's House, had gone down into the cellars to get some coke for the solid fuel stove.

John Mitchell made a tape of what she said, and this is how it went. "I was aware of someone coming from behind. I was petrified. I curled up waiting to see what would happen. The dog wouldn't come down the stairs, and stood at the top crying, which never happened before. I was in the first long passage leading to the cellars. I slowly looked behind, and saw four, or five horses being led – they looked completely solid, but very weary, and very dirty. I couldn't see any legs or feet on either the horses or the humans."

The witness added: "I did see it two or three other times – sometimes they were mostly all on the horses, sometimes leading them. They were all very, very dirty and splashed with mud as if they'd had a long journey – with the soldiers leaning on the horse's necks as if they were asleep. I had never heard of the Roman ghosts before I saw them the first time."

This lady approached Mr Mitchell to tell him of her experience after hearing a public lecture by him on the subject. He was surprised and pleased to discover another person claiming a similar sighting. However since the information was volunteered after the lecture – and not before the details of Harry's sighting became known to her, there is the inevitable suspicion that the account, although different, could have been fabricated. All I can add is that both Harry and the lady sound like genuine witnesses to the listener, and neither was willing to accept elaborations or additions to their stories prompted by their questioners.

However, Harry's was by far the superior account of the two, with tremendous detail, which provides the basis for believing him. The lady's account is interesting also, because it is a variation of Harry's tale, with the action occurring in another part of the cellars, and involving more horses, some of which were led, rather than ridden. What is interesting is that the apparitions in each case seem to have been coming from the same direction in relation to the witness – roughly, as far as I can gauge, from the North. This is the direction often associated in mythology with the realms of the dead. According to archaeologist, and the pioneer of pendulum divination, T.C. Lethbridge, North was associated with blackness, cold, and death. And the Romans are most certainly dead, probably pretty cold, and likely to be coming from a very dark place.

It it interesting to note that the haunted cellar is on a level with an ancient Roman by-way, the *Via Decumana*, which was roughly on the same alignment as the present Chapterhouse Street, outside Treasurer's

House. Therefore the mansion straddles a major military thoroughfare, leading from the North East gate in the Roman city wall – the direction from which most barbarian attacks would proceed – to the *Principa,* or Roman military headquarters building, the foundations of which can still be seen, situated in the freshly-excavated Undercroft of York Minster. Down here, among unearthly shadows cast by the modern floodlighting, the visitor may inspect the remains of part of the greatness that was Rome. Busts of long-dead emperors gaze sombrely from plinths, over the low, uneven masonry, which composed the Principa foundations, the angles of which are strangely at odds with the alignment of the Minster. Here was heard the rough bark of orders in a foreign tongue, when soldiers from Spain, Gaul, the Mediterranean lands, as well as Italy, marshalled about their business. Inside the Principa, with its lofty ceilings balanced above immense stone columns, the important business of empire was conducted. The York Principa was at one time the military headquarters for the whole of Roman Britain. The Emperor Constantine was proclaimed here, and both Hadrian and Severus knew it as their headquarters in Britain. The Undercroft of the Minster has a strangely oppressive ambience. A deadening of external noise, and the barely detectable aroma of dust and death from past centuries could be to blame, in part, for the robed figures seen by Minster guides.

The past becomes quickly buried in York. Layer upon layer of archaeological debris accumulated with the passing of each subsequent age within the confines of the city walls as older dwellings fell and decayed – or were demolished, levelled out and built upon again. For a long time the Principa was a large decaying stone edifice, apparently avoided as an accursed, or haunted place, by the early Anglian settlers in York. The evidence for this is the wide curve of Goodramgate, one of the city's oldest streets, said to have been originally directed around the extensive Roman ruins. The Anglo-Saxons had a well-recorded superstitious fear of deserted Roman sites. And why not, when one considers some of the deities they were in the habit of worshipping – grim Nemesis, the goddess of vengeance to whom the gladiators made obeisance, in chilling Nemesiums, small chambers, set aside, at the edge of the amphitheatre where the masses revelled in blood-sports, and the gladiators met their destinies. More sinister yet was Hecate, originally a Greek goddess, having power over the dead and the underworld, the bloody she-who-comes-from-afar, the sender of ghosts and demons. Patroness of witches and sorcery, Hecate was sometimes worshipped in deep caves, or underground chambers, her demons were said to have some peculiarity of the feet, which necessitated concealment, and she was associated with horses, leading the wild hunt of spirits of the dead through the stormy sky. Of her followers she demanded blood sacrifice, and foul invocations, summoning all the bestial side of human nature. She was thought to appear at crossroads on moonlit nights, and sacrifices were made to her there. Sometimes columns were erected to her in such places, and acted as her shrine, from which she was invoked ...

One wonders if such shrines still exist, beneath the streets of York, or whether the stray column in the cellar of Treasurer's House might have been dedicated to the goddess, and whether the strange happenings there, could be an archaic remnant of Hecate, patroness of horse riders, who was worshipped at crossing, forks, and parting of ways, chiefly at the end of the fourth century AD!

Having studied all the evidence from Harry Martindale's account, we decided to do something practical to prove or disprove, explain, or make more certain, what was going on in the dark and empty cellars of Treasurer's House.

Bob Staniforth and I had been very impressed by Harry's story, and the unshakeable manner in which he stood in the cellar where it happened, and repeated the experience. While he and I talked, Bob took pictures. We were not to know then that we would become very familiar with that cellar – spending more time there, probably, than anyone since the workmen who built it.

With the permission of the National Trust, who own the house, we were allowed regularly into the cellars, usually in the day-time, although during the winter months, frequently after it had gone dark outside – not that this made much difference to the lighting conditions in the cellar, which, without electric light, is pitch black.

The first thing we did was to gather together two electronics experts with an interest in the subject, Tom Anderson, and Eric Andrews. They provided a variety of equipment to record any movements by physical objects in the cellar.

On our first visit to install equipment we were mystified by a large silvered glass ball, with mirrored surface, which, nestling in a cardboard box, was the only occupant of the cellar, stuck away in a corner. I subsequently learned that such balls were termed spirit glasses, and were thought in former times to absorb evil humours, and were often placed, on this account, in the rooms of sick people. But who put this one in the cellar, or when, remained a mystery. In the meantime, we peered hopefully into its distorting reflections – although determining quietly to keep to scientific methods, we were not averse to the odd psychic long-shot.

In a corner of the locked cellar, investigators found this silvered ball – known as a "spirit glass", thought to draw away malignant influences such as diseases in former times. No-one could say who put it there.

The first equipment we installed was a sound-activated tape recorder. Eric Andrews designed and built two sound activation devices which would switch on the recorder whenever anything audible occurred. The first device was not sufficiently sensitive, so the first two weeks of tapes were not very useful. But the second worked perfectly, and with the first week's tape we checked, something unusual was discovered. We began recording in about November, so the vital winter period, when the phenomena usually seemed to occur, would be covered. We were both pleased, and mystified, when, apart from the metallic chinks we had recorded on earlier tapes, there were other noises, which neither we, nor the Administrator of Treasurer's House could explain.

Among the sounds on the tape which *could* be identified, were footsteps of some heavy-footed person in the street above, and car horns on two occasions – followed by the roar of the passing vehicle. But there were other noises in the cellar, which had been locked, and unvisited for several days.

We recorded the definite, steady, and rhythmic beating of a kettle drum – a sound which started with military precision, continued fading slightly, and ended just as abruptly, after about a minute. There were also regular sounds of someone moving about, and a sound halfway between breathing, and the soft flop of sandals on a flat surface. At the time, the cellar floor was of uneven earth and stones, and when walked upon it made quite a different sound.

In an attempt to find a rational explanation I was invited by the Administrator to rhythmically bash the dustbins in the yard above the cellar. I tried it with my hands, and two pieces of wood, on the lids, the sides, and the inside of the bins, but none of us could make a noise like the drumming recorded in the cellar. Recorded and heard from below, the noise of the bins was barely audible, and much less drum-like. The only rational possibility remaining was that someone had deliberately entered the cellar with a drum, and performed a short military tattoo, for our benefit, as a joke – although the Administrator thought this unlikely, as he himself took a serious interest in the subject, and had instructed his staff to avoid disturbing the equipment.

We continued to monitor our results on a weekly basis, and sometime before February – the month which Harry had heard and seen the phenomena, over twenty years before, we recorded a single, lone, blast on what sounded like a foghorn. It was not a car horn, sounding deep, and throaty, like the horns on ships. We ruled out the possibility of a train horn, because the railway is too far from Treasurer's House. We were left only with conjecture, and the knowledge that deep throaty horns, similar to the Danish lur, were used in Roman military processions.

Our excitement mounted as February approached, but it was short-lived. During the vital month, our recording equipment developed a mysterious fault. The activating device switched on, and refused to switch off – wasting most of the tape on lots of nothing. Difficulties in getting replacements from the college meant the next stage of the operation – the installation of a sound-activated video camera, was also delayed. Finally, when we got it into the cellar, it proved a grave disappointment, as the device which switched it on was not very good, and had to be roused by a sharp whistle or handclap to switch on the floodlight, and start filming, even when we entered the room. All we achieved were interesting, but rather repetitious action replays of us entering and leaving the cellar – no Romans, or anyone else. What this proved, if anything, was how seldom anyone ever went in there.

We retained the equipment in the cellar well into the summer months, but removed it before the year was up. The results had been inconclusive, if interesting. They proved nothing, yet posed questions. Our own views at the time varied. My idea of some localised time warp gave way to theories of individual psychic receptivity and so on.

Bob Staniforth's idea, early in the experiment went: "In the cellar haunting I believe there is some kind of impression which is repeated every time conditions are right. Something occurs, which we know nothing about, to make it happen." His idea was similar to the theory of hauntings developed by T.C. Lethbridge, the Cambridge archaelogist. Bob thought that the very stones, or fabric of the cellar acted as a kind of recording medium, like the tape on a tape recorder, and was set in motion when the right conditions occurred, naturally. Lethbridge's similar idea was that the electromagnetic fields of streams, trees, rocks and so on, could be impressed with an image of something which had happened in the past, which they were capable of reproducing from time to time, when conditions were suitable. His further theory in relation to what he called ghouls, was that the tingling sensation in the limbs, and feeling of cold, was due to a draining of energy from the person experiencing the phenomena, because their own energy went to power the very happening they were experiencing. Lethbridge, however, put ghouls in a class of their own, as emotional feelings, of a destructive nature, which sometimes acted in a suggestible way on the minds of people experiencing them, which became impressed on the environment.

He gave an unpleasant example of an experience of his wife, who while walking on the cliffs on the south coast heard a voice say: "Why don't you jump?" and for a moment, she felt herself under a strange compulsion to comply, before returning to normal. Not long afterwards a man did commit suicide by jumping from that spot on the same cliffs. Lethbridge believed that the self-destructive urge was residual in the area, and had been, possibly, for an immense period of time, both as the harbinger, and memorial, of tragedies of the future as well as the past. Perhaps similar ideas about cliff tops are embodied in Manx stories of the little people, who lure men over the edge, after lying in wait for them.

Investigators and camera equipment. (Left-right, Eric Andrews, Steve Cliffe, Tom Anderson). Their equipment picked up inexplicable noises including a horn and drum beat

Apparently the Roman ghosts do not fall into this ghoulish category as there is no record of them actually harming anybody.

Tom Anderson, one of our electronics experts concluded: "We recorded something that we can't explain immediately – real sounds, made by things which aren't necessarily in that room, or seeming to relate to it. I would like to think it is a psychic happening. What we recorded might be time recordings."

Eric Andrews was the only convinced spiritualist among us. At the time he was ill with heart trouble, and died only a couple of years later of a heart attack at his home. His view was: "I have always believed in the manifestation of people after death. I believe there is something left when people die – some kind of energy that can reappear. It may be that dead people are at a different frequency than us. It's a matter of having a machine which can record at that frequency."

It was some years later before we returned to the cellar again, and this time, it was to test out another theory. Toying with the idea of a seven year recurrence of the phenomena, I had discovered that the seven year cycle of bad luck etc, was attributed by astrologers to the transits of the planet Uranus, which normally remained in each Zodiacal sign for seven years. I checked with an ephemeris, and discovered that Uranus changed signs shortly, so Tom, Bob, and I arranged to be in the cellar on the morning that the transit took place, at the exact time of the change-over.

The Administrator of Treasurer's House had laid on a reporter and photographer from the local evening paper, and we were interviewed and photographically recorded before descending into the bowels of the cellars for the last time. Bob had his camera, Tom had his tape recorder, and for extra effect, we switched off the light, and waited in the dark haunted cellar for the appointed moment. I cleared my mind, and tried to think of nothing. But strained ears and apprehension, or hope of something happening, mounted. After a while I kicked that wall close to where Harry had laid his ladder. I gave it three hefty kicks – perhaps, I reasoned, it had been Harry's hammering which had disturbed the ghosts, and set off the phenomena. Nothing happened. After a few moments, nothing continued to happen.

After a while we passed out into the sunshine again with inscrutable faces, and "no comment" for the waiting news-men. We ate an excellent lunch in an olde worlde Tudor restaurant, and went sight-seeing. By the evening I was beginning to feel rough, and I hadn't had anything but a single glass of wine to drink. At eight o'clock, I went to bed with a splitting headache and nausea, and began to feel like dying. I then developed what was the most baffling illness I have ever had. Before the night was through I was feverish, and had developed excruciating pains through the region of my back. It was agony to sit up, and for three days my only excursions were to the bathroom. I felt ineffably cold. When I could manage to hold up a book, I read about the frozen North of Canada to cheer me up – it seemed quite warm by comparison.

I never learned what I was suffering from – but I have subsequently been told that it could have been a severe inflammation of the spinal column, a very strange affliction to come down with so rapidly, and apparently without cause, or warning. Both Tom and Bob were OK, so my sudden illness seemed purely coincidental. I recovered, of course, after a while. But remembering Lethbridge's theories about energy drains, and Tom's remark, when we had been in the cellar for a while, that it seemed to be going colder suddenly, I have often wondered if the Romans came, but we didn't see them.

And whether they objected to me kicking their wall.

The remarkable feature of this haunting is the detail – possibly the finest sighting, detailed minutely, of any recorded apparition. Certainly in its subject, the Romans, it is one of the most interesting, throwing a spotlight on history almost, and bringing a bit of it back to life.

Neither witness knew of the haunting before their experiences, and neither was thrilled by it. Understandably, both were unwilling, for a very long time, even to admit to anyone that they had seen anything. This fact alone tends to confirm, rather than detract from the authenticity of their experiences.

Both witnesses noted that the legs of the soldiers and the horse, or horses, were not visible. Only in the excavated portion of the cellar, where archaeologists had been uncovering a Roman road, were the apparitions visible right down to their feet. This is an especially intriguing detail, as it implies a continuing correspondence of the ghostly soldiers to the exact ground level at the time of their actual earthly existence – at the end of the fourth century AD!

But the Romans were "known" to haunt the cellar, long before either witness knew of it. A former curator had several accounts of sightings in a book, which he showed to Harry, but which has disappeared. This is a common feature of a class of hauntings known as apparitions. Many people, over a protracted period, will have similar experiences in a certain place.

Later on, in the chapter "Explaining Ghosts", we will look at one current theory, thrown up by the developing science known as parapsychology, to 'explain' the phenomena.

6

THE LITTLE PEOPLE

"Supernormal beings, differing in type and character, but allied in race, who were once believed to inhabit this world, or a magical kingdom lying near, or below it."

That is how the *Encyclopedia Britannica* describes the fairies, or Little People, as they are sometimes known. Perhaps they do not seem a fit subject for a serious examination of supernatural phenomena, but their history is just as extensive as that of ghosts. And even today, in our sophisticated electronic era, of computers and space shuttles, we are never so far from our roots in nature that some of us are not aware of something else, living with us, but just below, or beyond, the bounds of our perception. "They", however, may be more gifted, having "the second sight", and may have seen something very old and inexplicable, defying the relations of time, and having the same source as other supernatural phenomena.

Fairies were believed in former times to be akin to men in many respects. The relatively recent prettying of their image in children's stories overlays an older, and more sinister tradition. Far from the tiny tinsel-like creatures of nursery stories, the original fairies were solid, and in many cases, as large as adult human beings, with whom they intermarried, and had children.

The fairies were not human, nor were they higher spirits, but sometimes thought of as, "of middle nature, between men and angels". The medieval Christian church did not distinguish between them and demons. Both were regarded as evil spirits. The Anglo-Saxon fairy was an "elf", while Welsh legend attributed fairies to the souls of Druids, who, not being Christian, could not enter heaven, and roamed about, performing mischief instead. A modern-day goblin, seen by airmen when the oxygen is low in high-flying aircraft is the gremlin, variously described as a little animal, or dwarf, seen scurrying about, and usually blamed for any technical hitches.

Might the "little people" be the spirits of virtuous druids?

The original fairies were said to be skilled in magic, able to change shape at will, make themselves invisible, and enchant human beings, in whose lives they often interfered for good or evil.

They were thought to live much longer than men, but when they died they perished utterly, having no souls.

Belief in fairies exists in many parts of the world. They have been traditionally feared as dangerous and powerful beings, sometimes friendly to men, but often cruel or mischievous. It was considered better not to speak of them by name, as this gave them power over the speaker, and they had to be referred to by euphemisms such as "the gentle people", or "the good neighbours", and indeed, the Scottish brownie was thought of as a helpful household spirit.

Green was the chosen colour of the fairies, and it was considered unwise for humans to wear it. There are Celtic people today who believe that green is an unlucky colour. I know of a mother who warned her son that a pair of green cord trousers he bought would prove unlucky. The next day he came off his motorbike. Psychological suggestion, or sheer coincidence may have been the explanation, but he never wore them again after the accident.

It was also unlucky to frequent places known to be haunted by fairies, and those who visited fairyland sometimes returned with addled wits, drained of vitality, and even died soon after. Others lost all sense of time, thinking they had been away for only a few short hours, they found years had elapsed, their friends were dead, and they were dimly remembered as someone lost, inexplicably, long ago. Those visitors who ate food in fairyland never returned.

Fairies were thought to steal from humans whilst invisible, and sickly, malformed changeling children were substituted by fairies for healthy human ones, so that the fairy child could benefit from human milk. These fairies were usually normal human size or slightly smaller. But others were only the size of small children, or smaller still.

There were said to be fairy treasures, fairy islands, fairy cauldrons, fairy cups, fairy horns – some of which came into the possession of humans, and can still be seen today.

The strangest of all, perhaps, were the fairy wives, who married humans on condition of a special promise being exacted from them. One such was the fairy wife of Wild Edric, an Anglo-Saxon folk hero, who lived in Shropshire, in the time of William the Conqueror. He married a fairy from the forest of Clun, in Shropshire, who promised to be a good wife on condition that he did not upbraid her on her fairy origins. When he eventually did so, in a domestic argument, she returned to her people forever.

A similar tale comes from Wales. In the 12th century a young farmer was startled by the appearance of three beautiful women, who emerged from a small lake, Llyn-y-Fan-Fach, which still exists today near Llandeusant in Carmarthenshire. He fell in love with one, and after correctly identifying her from her sisters, a year later, her father agreed to his marrying her on condition that, "you never give her three needless blows, in anger or in play, and that you never touch her with iron, or she will return to me, and bring in her wake all her possessions." The fairy father gave a handsome dowry of sheep, goats, cattle and horses, and the farmer and his fairy lived near the village of Myddfai, where she bore him three sons. But he struck his wife twice – once because she laughed at a funeral, and once because she wept at a wedding. He vowed not to strike her again, but one day, as she helped him to harness some oxen to the plough, he accidentally caught her with the iron bit of a bridle. "You have struck the last blow. Farewell!" So saying, she turned, and summoning her animals, she disappeared into the lake, and the animals with her. The cries and entreaties of her distracted husband were to no avail, and he drowned in the lake, trying to follow her. Later her sons followed the deep furrow, made by the oxen harnessed to the plough, right to the edge of the lake. Here their mother rose from the waters, and spoke to them. She told the eldest that he must become a healer, and with fairy lore, he became the first of a long line of famous physicians of Myddfai, known throughout Wales for their skill.

There are various theories to account for the legends of fairies, but they comprise three main ideas. These are chiefly that the fairies, or little people, represent an ancestor, or folk memory of ancient neolithic peoples, or that they are a memory of a belief in nature spirits or pagan gods, or that fairies are the souls of the ancient dead.

First, the idea that our ancestors may have come into contact with a much older stone age culture, and smaller, primitive people, living precariously in isolated communities in the woods or wastes, is supposed to explain the fairies' affinity for nature. Knowledge of the countryside, and living close to nature in remote places might have led to a belief in the magical powers of the little people to survive in impossible places. Also intermarriage, robbings, kidnappings and child-swopping, would not have been an impossibility between races, if the fairies were of normal, or only slightly smaller size.

The idea that fairies were dethroned pagan gods, or nature spirits, whose worship was suppressed by the coming of Christianity, is also interesting. Before Europe was Christianised, pagan man held a general belief that all the wonders of creation were ruled by systems and degrees of gods and spirits – a belief in common with the ancient practice of shamanism, which aimed at controlling what happened through the invoking of spirits. In Ireland the leprechaun was considered a solitary nature spirit of the remote places. In Scotland kelpies haunted moors and woods, while in England, Jenny Greenteeth was a water sprite, who haunted rivers, and lonely waterways, waiting to lure the unwary to a watery end.

Some wood and water fairies seem to preserve memories of classical mythological beings such as fauns, goat-footed creatures with human bodies, dryads, mysterious tree sprites, and nereids, spirits of streams and water. Displaced pagan gods crop up in the form of supernatural people, like the Twylwyth Teg in Wales, and the Daoine Sidhe, in Ireland.

The Twylwyth Teg (the Fair Family or Folk) of Wales were sometimes said to be departed druids, who lived on invisible fairy islands in the sea. On moonlit nights the Twylwyth Teg would dance in fairy rings in the fields. Rings of toadstools or mushrooms marked the spot in the morning.

Fairies are often associated with ancient burial mounds. In Ireland, the Tuatha De were believed to have been given overlordship of the underworld there, and the places of their chiefs were the green grassy mounds, which dotted the land. Fairyland was an underground region, according to many folktales, and had certain resemblances to the kingdom of the dead. The known dead were sometimes seen in fairyland, and in a Cornish tale "The Fairy Dwelling of Selena Moor", it is explicitly stated that the fairies are in fact, the dead.

Obviously all these sources have become inextricably interwoven in folklore, adding to, and confusing the attributes and origins of a belief in the existence of some personalised, semi-human representation of the raw spirit of nature.

It seems likely that our forefathers, if they encountered a small, primitive and secret people, perhaps surviving in small bands in forests and inaccessible places of desolation, where no-one else wished to settle, attributed their mysterious survival to magic, and considered them supernatural beings, when in fact they were merely human.

I know that in Cheshire I have seen arrow heads which were found embedded in the trunks of trees cut down only in the last century. They are known locally as "elf bolts". Now it may be that the use of flint arrow heads as a cheap form of weapon for hunting continued among later peoples, until the time that these ancient oaks were young trees. But it is also possible that the primitive neolithic peoples continued more numerously in closed communities into much later times than historians have previously suspected. Certainly until the early middle ages the forests of Cheshire and the wastes of the Pennine moors, near where these arrowheads were fired, would have provided ample refuge for nomadic hunters, living in small bands.

It is very likely, however, that experiences of neolithic people only added to an already-existing belief in nature spirits, which, in turn, became associated with any object arousing superstitious awe in our ancestors, such as the ancient burial mounds and stone circles which they encountered in the settlement of an alien island.

An interesting folk legend concerned the haunting of a burial mound in Clwyd, North Wales, by a golden man, or fairy. This belief had persisted for generations. When the mound was finally excavated a beautiful cloak, made from thin discs of gold, rivetted together, was discovered enshrouding the disintegrated remains of its ancient owner.

Several accounts exist, including this one, written by John Langford:
"The gold breast-plate, now in my possession, was raised on the 11th of October 1833 from a rough vault in a field in my farm (about a quarter of a mile from the town) called Bryn-yr-Ellyllon. The stones had partially fallen in, among which were found bones of a man, and the breast-plate, which was partly bent together from the weight of the stones which had fallen on it. The discovery happened by removing what appeared to be a mass of litter, in order to level the mound with the rest of the field. About three or four hundred loads of pebbles and other stones were found upon the place where the body had apparently been laid"

A Miss Angharad Llwyd, daughter of the rector of Caerwys wrote in 1835:

"The field in which this curious piece of antiquity was found is near Mold, and known by the name of 'Cae Ellyllon' (The Field of Goblyns) from stories handed down from one generation to another, caused by the appearance of a man of gigantic size, having been seen on several occasions, standing on a Tumulus, in the said field, through which there is a common path; many a well authenticated tale has been told, by old and young of the fright occasioned by the appearance of this formidable golden spectre. Mr. Clough, Vicar of Mold, Mr. Hughes, surgeon, Miss Wynne, Mr. Williams an intelligent agent to Mr. Cooke and another gentleman, have heard the 'golden spectre' given as a reason, by women and children, why they would not walk through Cae Ellyllon after dusk.

In 1833 Mr. John Langford, perpetual overseer of the roads, who rents the field, set ten men to dig up the Tumulus for stone to mend the roads; towards the lower part, they found some very large bones – a skull of greater than the usual size of man – and a bright corslet with 2 or 300 amber beads, the bones became dust, on being exposed the the air. Sr. W. W. Wynn and Mr. Hesketh of Gwrych, both men above the ordinary stature found the corslet too large for them. Mr. Langford told Mr. Newcome, Warden of Ruthin, in my presence, that he remembers having heard about 25 years ago, that a female was leading home her drunken husband through the Goblyn field, when they saw the Golden Spectre standing on the Tommen, which scared the woman into fits and the man into sobriety, he and Mr. Hughes the surgeon say that Nancy (who died in June 1834) used to affirm constantly that she saw the same object on the very same spot 14 years ago when fetching home Mr. Langford's cows, one moon-light night; this, she told so soon as she got into the house, and she enjoyed the idea of having lived to hear on her dying bed that the 'ghost was raised'. Mrs. Hughes and her son announced it to her. Mr. Langford and many others declare that they know a dress-maker who has been crazed for the last seven years in consequence of having seen the apparition, when returning home late at night. 'It was,' she said, 'glittering and shining in gold.' These and similar anecdotes are current in the neighbourbood."

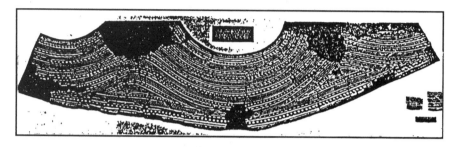

The gold corslet of Mold (British Museum)

The corslet, which was covered in rows of small beads of resin-like amber, and the remains of a serge-type cloth, was initially flung aside by Langford as of no value and pieces were broken off as keepsakes by curious onlookers. Apart from the bones of the corslet's owner, a barrow-load of burnt bones and ashes were uncovered about two to three yards away, which turned out to be human remains. There was also a quantity of iron rust, or copper, which crumbled to dust on being touched.

After the corslet became an exhibit, at the British Museum, it was thought that the unusual size could be attributed to its use as a peytrel, or brunt for a pony. But later analysis suggests that this bronze age cape, as it is now listed, was indeed intended for a man.

A museum expert told me: "It is probably early to middle bronze age, about 1600 years BC, and as a shoulder cape for a man would have been worn with a backing of leather or fur. In the gallery it is shown modelled on human shoulders and fits quite well. Although it has some superficial resemblance to other pieces, it is actually unique in Europe." The expert insisted that it was the product of a definitely pre-Celtic culture.

The thin gold plate is embosed in a style seen on bucklers from Wales and elsewhere, but with a rich variety of patterns including circular bosses of two sizes, pyramidal rivet heads, pointed ovals and quadrangular bosses separated by simple raised lines. It is similar to the illustration of a Druid's corslet, supposedly based on an Irish late bronze age gorget, as drawn by S.R. Meyrick and C.H. Smith in 1815 – nearly 20 years before this one was dug up. (See illustration of druid page 51).

The medieval church did not distinguish between fairies and demons, and it is still difficult to make the distinction, in the old sense of both, as simply different forms of the spirits of nature. Fairies seem, however, to be more connected with natural things, like vegetation and water. They are also regarded as somewhat more enchanting and benign, as the contemporary view of a demon is that of a hideous monster, or, according to biblical definition, a fallen angel, which had chosen to attach itself to Satan. But more of this in the next chapter. What I want to consider here are the contemporary experiences of people, known personally to me, who have unexpectedly had some contact with "the little people."

It may be surprising to some readers, and even a little intriguing, to learn that one Scottish academic professor has made a serious study of numerous sightings of fairies, or small people in green, seen by many different people throughout Scotland, the North of England, and what he defines broadly as, "the Celtic areas." All of them seem to have general features in common, as do those which I shall now relate.

The first story concerns a little girl of Manx parentage. She was born in a small village on Curragh – marshland, once under sea – in the north of the island. She and her parents lived in a converted sergeant's mess on what had been a wartime airfield. This was a wooden building which had been taken over by the local council to provide temporary housing for returned servicemen and their families. One night the little girl was allowed a sip of her father's Guinness before going to bed. Some time in the night she was roused from sleep by a strange glow in the room, which seemed to come from under the bed. Craning over, she leaned down to look, and beheld a curious sight (the side of her cot was left folded down, so she could wriggle over the edge to see).

Underneath her cot were four or five little men, illuminated by the light. They were holding hands in a circle and walking round, in an anti-clockwise direction with a slow step. Most were bearded, with dark hair, and brown leathery caps, like round hoods, flush with the head, and having chin flaps. One of them had dark red hair, and was clean shaven, and wasn't wearing a hat. Their clothes consisted of simple loose tunics, some green, some brown, tied around with a belt at the waist, and their leggings were loose, again, in either green or brown – usually brown tunic and green leggings, or green tunic and brown leggings. They were of normal proportionate adult human build, and seemed quite occupied with what they were doing, and oblivious of the child. Since they appeared to fit under the cot, so that their heads just reached the top, it seems they must have been about 18 inches high.

The little girl was convinced that she was not dreaming. She called to her mother, who switched on the light, and, of course, when she tried to show her where the little people were, they had gone.

In all the years since, the little girl, now a grown woman, and mother of children herself, has insisted that what she saw was not a dream. Naturally, the Guinness has taken a large part of the blame for what she saw, but despite the rib tickling she discounts this theory, and sticks by the reality of the details impressed on her mind.

What does she think they were? "Little people, with a reality of their own," and, that they were somehow, "connected with the earth." The little girl associated the experience with her subsequent liking for the smell of raw freshly turned earth. She does not claim to know, one way or the other, what they might have been, and has no particular belief in fairies.

However, there is a long-established belief in fairies among the people of the Isle of Man. At one bridge in the island, near Castletown, one is expected to greet, "the little people" when crossing, or bad luck will follow. And a well-known poem of the island contains the verse:

"Up the Eirey mountain, and down the Rushen glen;
We cannot go a-hunting, for fear of little men."

This was thought to refer to malevolent sprites, who lay in wait among the rocks and clefts of the cliff-tops, to lure huntsmen to their doom.

A former colleague of mine had a similar experience to that of the little girl, when he was about four or five years old. He remembers that he had been playing with this father in the front room, running out into the lobby, or hall-way to the front door, which was quite dark, since it was night time, and the light was switched off, he was surprised to see a group of small figures at the far end of the lobby, near the front door, seemingly illuminated by a strange light. They were wearing vaguely medieval-type costumes, in browns and greens. Some had caps on, some had leggings or high boots. They also had a small pack animal with them, laden with baggage, either a mule or a donkey.

Although he was so young, my colleague is adamant that what he saw was not a dream. He says that he was old enough to realise that the people, who seemed to be only inches high, were not really physically there – but that it was some sort of projection of an image. He felt perturbed by them, but not terrified – uneasy that they seemed to be aware of him, shouting and gesticulating towards him, in a jeering or fun-poking way. There seemed to be a gulf between him and them, as if they were in another dimension, different from, but possibly existing alongside our own. To the little boy they felt alien – not necessarily evil, but unsettling, and to be kept at a distance. Running to his father, he tried to tell him what he had seen. In later years, his father also admitted to a similar experience when he was young, but on this occasion, he saw nothing. It transpired that many members of this family had psychic experiences of one kind or another, and there was said to be at least one, so gifted, in every generation.

At the time of his experience, my friend was living in a northern industrial town, on the fringe of the Pennine hills, Oldham, and it was when he was living in another town, not far away, that his own daughter had a similar experience.

This little girl saw a green man, who flew, or floated into the bedroom, and started to ask her questions. Her father had never spoken previously of his own sighting, and there was no question of it being a case of suggestion. The child insisted, and has insisted ever since, that what happened was real, and not a dream.

So what is the explanation? My friend is an educated man, with a public position, and unlikely to want to undermine his own credibility – which is why I don't give his name. The lady from the Isle of Man is similarly intelligent, with analytical ability. Both are baffled by the experience, yet both retain an almost fierce determination that what happened was real. How many more of us, with similar tales to tell, must there be?

My own idea, as a person who has never seen either fairies or ghosts, is that a kind of unconscious suggestion is at work. It is possible to over-analyse phenomena of this kind, and as life, like religion, is basically an illogical act of faith, in which we hope, or believe that there is something purposeful, perhaps such experiences have a special meaning of their own, and fall into a similar category. To some people the actual daily business of living, acquiring one's daily bread, and pursuing everyday aims, is an end in itself. But for others, there has to be something further, some ultimate meaning, purpose, or goal to all the striving. Belief in the mysterious, or inexplicable is part of this need.

The controversial psychologist, C.G. Jung, whose works are held by some to be more art than science, had something to say of spirits, and little people. The spirit seen in dreams and folklore he believed was a symbolic representation of the evolution and growth of the life force in the individual. "Little People", were sometimes broken-off independent complexes in the psyche with an autonomous volition of their own. The unconscious mind of the individual recognised this by representing their potentially dangerous, mischievous, and unpredictable qualities in the form of elves, sprites and so on. Although small, they had the magical power to do things which were "supernatural," that is, wreak havoc in the psyche, unless they could be integrated in some way, as part of the whole personality.

He also spoke of the colour green as usually appearing in the dreams and visions of his patients as a "vegetation numen", being symbolic of the healing, or growing qualities of nature. He also associated it with the sensation function, which is most closely connected with an individual's relation to the physical world through the senses of sight, hearing, taste, touch, smell and so on. In some persons, this function is severely underdeveloped, and is largely unconscious, where it becomes mixed up, and tainted with all the fantastic contents of dreams, fantasies, and infantile feelings. In mild forms of schizophrenia dream-like visions often intrude on normal conscious vision and hearing. This is most commonly seen in delirious children during the course of feverish illnesses, and I know one adult, who went through a paranoid phase of believing himself followed by little people, whilst a teenager. However, Jung himself was the first to recognise that the irrational played as big a part, though an underestimated and largely unrecognised one, as all the sensible, concrete, works of man, in the life of us humans.

Sometimes, I have noticed, while walking in lonely country lanes, with the thickly-grown hedgerows of early summer clustering on both sides, and the buzz of tired insects at eventide, a strange extra "something", the feeling of a force, a sentient being, an unseen "watcher", whom, if one were fast enough, one might catch a glimpse of, by glancing quickly round. And I have felt the brooding presence, charged with menace, hanging mistily over the running brook, as one hastily crosses a bridge in a deep, dark, clough, as the dusky nights of late autumn drawn in.

And I have experienced the enchantment of hidden and secret places, and mossy caves, where the loudest sound, the echoing drip of water, has a magic of its own.

These are our own experiences. Why devalue them by saying too much ... ?

7

A MODERN-DAY
DEMON

Will was an experienced evangelical minister of a fundamentalist Christian church, with a missionary brief. His job was to go out and find
people who might benefit from the message of the bible. His church had
sent him on assignment to a remote part of North Wales – the Lleyn
peninsula, which in those days, the 1930s, was known only for one
phenomenon – Lloyd George, the Welsh Wizard, the great ex-premier,
whose wizardry extended only to politics, and women.

Will, a young man with no interest in politics, was about to discover
wizardry of a different kind. He understood the biblical injunction
against such practices in Deuteronomy, which rules that spirit mediums,
spell-casters, and conjurors of demons should, "not be found among
you". Lloyd George did not fall into this category, although his political
opponents might have thought so, and apart from being a local hero, he
has no bearing on this story.

Pressing the case of his relatively modern church in a backward
region, with an ingrained Methodist tradition, was hard work for Will
the young Englishman, so he was glad to find a potential convert in a
young woman who lived alone – her mother having recently died. Bible
readings were instituted at the young woman's house, and Will took
along his wife, May.

After the first bible study Will and May left some literature about
their church, and it was while reading this that the young Welsh woman
was startled by ornaments moving on the mantelpiece. She mentioned
this to Will and May the next time they called. At first they were
dubious, but on the third occasion they visited her, she was quite upset,
saying that things had got much worse. They began the reading, and
had not gone very far when the woman's words were vindicated.
Ornaments on the mantelpiece started to move. They slid with quite
deliberate movements, as if pushed by an unseen hand, until they

toppled with a loud crash into the hearth. Pictures started to shake on the walls, and one or two suddenly leapt, or were propelled, by some force, two or three feet into the room.

Gargoyles leer and squat on the tower of Brookfield Church, Manchester. Intended to frighten away malignant spirits, they took on a demonic aspect in medieval times and were included by Victorian craftsmen, even on Non-conformist chapels.

The Lleyn has always been regarded in Welsh folklore as, "the place where the soul finds peace." It reaches out like a questing arm, or tentacle, from the high mountains of Snowdonia into the mysterious and legend-shrouded waters of the Irish Sea. The sea into which the secret and sinister brotherhood of Druids departed when the Romans came.

The sea in which the invisible islands of the Twylwyth Teg are thought to be situated. A sea also of drowned lands, and lost cities, mythical monsters, mermaids, and sea serpents.

Faced with the seemingly-impossible, the young minister was shaken. All the forces latent in imagination and nightmares seemed to be gathering to oppose his mission. All the authority of ancient legend and the superstition of the past challenged him, rising up in his own mind, threatening to overwhelm sanity and reason. But he had to show faith, and give the guidance of reason. He put aside his own fears, and incomprehension, to cleave by the only answer he knew, and the only one which could help the young woman.

Whilst the unearthly chaos continued, the minister led the two women in prayer. The noise subsided. When all was quiet, Will asked the woman if she had ever been involved with spiritualism. She had not, but she remembered that her mother was, in fact, a spiritualist medium, and had held seances in the house, in that very room. He asked if anything remained of her mother's connected with this practice, and the woman replied that a number of books on the subject were in the house.

Will's advice was simple. In the Acts of the Apostles, books on witchcraft and mediumship are burned. His view was that the disturbance was a demonic influence centering on the books. Together, the three collected the offending material, and consigned it to the fire, and, as Will tells it, from that time on, the disturbance ceased, and the young woman became a full member of the church.

Will is now an elderly gentleman, and still a respected minister of the same church. He sometimes mentions his experience in Wales as an illustration of the real, and tangible power of evil.

I mention his story – at the risk of offending spiritualists everywhere – as a classic example of poltergeist phenomena, as such disturbances are known. Whether Will was correct in his prognosis, I do not know, but something they did must have been right. I have no doubt that spiritualists reading this book will have other ideas on how it should have been tackled. It is unlikely that Will or other members of his church will ever read this, but in giving his first-hand account, I have not revealed the identity of either, and no harm will be done to reputations, individual or collective.

But is a poltergeist a demon? My own experiences of this type of phenomena are limited to the sudden, and questionable, occurrence of astonishing incidents at a working men's club in Huddersfield. It was not actually on, but just after, April fool's day, when a photographer and I went to the club-house, a large grimy Victorian building near the modern ring road. In the overly high and draughty passageways of this badly-conceived edifice, rejoicing in the name of Huddersfield Friendly and Trades Club, and, even at that time, considered to be falling down through traffic vibration, we met a pasty and chastened collection of domestic staff. Yes, something really weird was happening. It had happened on two nights. Bottles behind the bar had crashed off shelves. Glasses had tippled over, and beer pumps had gone on of their own accord. One customer sitting at a table had dodged a shower of beer bottles which flew across the bar.

Looking backwards and forwards among the faces I detected only looks of concern – no muffled sniggers, or barely concealed smiles in sight. I pointed out the close proximity of April Fool's day. Oh, no, no! It wasn't a joke. All this had really happened. And there, just across the bar, in an upper room, complete with staring eyes, was a little nine-year-old boy. Yes, it's funny. He had been thinking about the pumps just before they came on – and the beer bottles, and the glasses. Why wasn't he at school? He's too upset. Where is the evidence? Oh, we've cleared it up.

Although the story got into print, there were no follow-ups. A councillor on the clubs' management committee rang up the editor, and my trip to monitor the poltergeist was called off. I rang the staff at the club later, to see if anything further had occurred, but possibly, like editors, even poltergeists obey the injunctions of borough councillors. The startling, disturbing, manifestations, had ended as abruptly and mysteriously as they began.

In fact, a poltergeist does not seem to be regarded as quite the same thing as a demon, although they may have certain manifestations in common. A poltergeist is literally a "noisy spirit" and constitutes one of the two major forms of haunting – the other being that of apparitions. Characteristic poltergeist behaviour usually begins with unexplained noises – notably of a percussion type, raps, thuds, bangs, drum beats (!), galloping hooves etc. They are normally centred round, and dependant on, the presence of a young girl or adolescent youth – although sometimes the agent may be an adult. Sounds are often of falling objects crashing to the ground, but frequently the damage done is small compared with the commotion heard. Violent bed shaking is a very common symptom of poltergeist activity, and sometimes the whole bed and its occupant is lifted into the air, falling back with a bone-jarring crash.

Other alleged phenomena are the movement of objects thrown through the air, but often moving so slowly, their course can be followed clearly. The appearance of objects from inside a locked room, mysterious patches of water, or oil, spontaneous fires, and occasional voices are also associated with poltergeist hauntings. Stone throwing here, has attained a category of its own, with reports of the phenomena from all parts of the world, agreeing so closely in detail, as to cast little doubt on the validity of the incidents.

Poltergeist disturbances have been recorded from very early times. Harry Price in his book, "Poltergeist Over England" cited many mentions by classical authors and early historians.

In England, during the period of early religious ferment occasioned by the First Civil War, a curious case came to light in what is now an urban, industrialised district of Manchester. The Duckenfields of Dukinfield Hall, were a radical Puritan family who allowed their family chapel to be used as a meeting place by members of an Independent religious faction. They were followers of a fiery preacher, Samuel Eaton, who had been ejected from his rectorship of West Kirby in the Wirral for his unconventional preaching. Eaton had been jailed in London as a "schismatical and dangerous fellow", before going over to Puritan colonies in New England. He returned to Britain with the intention of gathering about him potential settlers for a new Puritan colony in Connecticut, but the Civil War had begun and things began to look up for the Puritans of England.

Robert Duckenfield owned the chapel where the phantom drum was heard.

Eaton started to preach to his Independent congregation at the invitation of Colonel Duckenfield, a young officer in the Parliamentary army, who made him chaplain to the regiment stationed about Stockport Parish. Cromwell was at this time purging the army of officers and soldiers who belonged to any other

than the Independent persuasion in order to weld a tight-knit, per-
sonally-loyal fighting force. Duckenfield later became one of his leading
officers and a member of the Council of State.

*Dukinfield Old Chapel as it was and now, as a devastated ruin standing in a
builder's yard. It is the site of the oldest recorded poltergeist haunting in
England and there are plans to restore it as a Civil War Museum.*

The old chapel at Dukinfield, whose ruins now stand in a modern industrial estate, became the setting for perhaps the earliest recorded poltergeist phenomena in the country. It is described in the history of the chapel thus:

"Moreover in the summer of 1646, there had occurred a mysterious incident in the Chapel at the Old Hall, which had roused much attention, and had been thought to presage that the Independents were "greedy of a warre," which would "prove their ruine." As Master Eaton was preaching, there was heard the perfect sound as of a man beating a march on a drum; and it was heard as coming into the chappel, and then going up all along the ile through the people, and so about the chappel, but nothing seen; which Master Eaton, preaching, and the people that sate in the several parts of the chappel, heard; insomuch that it terrified Master Eaton, and the people caused him to give over preaching and fall to praying; but, the march still beating, they broke up their exercise for that time, and were glad to be gone." – Gaingraena iii,164.

There was no immediate explanation or result and the following year the Chapel was visited by the young George Fox, founder of the Quaker movement. It is recorded that here was the first place he, "declared truth", that is, preached a sermon. But by all accounts it did not go down well as he advocated a pure and sinless life. Ultimately, the Independents were suppressed and most of the work of Cromwell and his army was undone.

But the first detailed poltergeist haunting was that of, "the drummer of Tedworth" – written about by the Rev Joseph Glanvill in 1681.

Some years before, in 1661, to be precise, a magistrate of Tedworth caused the arrest of a vagrant drummer, and confiscated his drum. What exactly a vagrant drummer is, I don't know, but let us assume he was an unemployed ex-soldier, at a loose end, as the civil wars were now ended – with the restoration of Charles II. Anyway, about a month after the drummer's imprisonment , the magistrate's family began to be plagued by thumping and drumming noises – first on the roof of their house, and later inside it. Things got progressively worse, with scratchings, lifting of the children's beds, and movement of floorboards. These and other phenomena continued for months, and were witnessed by many people. "of repute and intelligence." Although the Rev Glanvill's account may have been exaggerated, the sworn statement by the magistrate, describing the phenomena, probably merely reflected his agitation in the face of the unknown. What happened to the soldier I don't know. He may have been released. At all events the drumming stopped. Was it due to the drummer – or did a spontaneous phenomena, perhaps associated with the magistrate's children merely prick his conscience, and point towards that cause? Or was it trickery, or a practical joke, which got out of hand – with hysteria and suggestibility as the result? We are unlikely ever to know.

Another famous case affected the Wesley family. The Rev Samuel Wesley, the father of John Wesley, the founder of Methodism, wrote about it in family letters. The manifestations seemed to centre around Hetty Wesley, John's sister, who was a nineteen-year-old girl at the time. They consisted of noises of great variety and loudness, including one, "like a stone thrown among many bottles," and also, the appearance of, "a vague shape." The disturbances lasted for about a year before they petered out.

These two, one in the seventeenth, the other in the eighteenth century, are fairly early cases, but there are many others, from all over the world, centering on children, young women, and even adults of either sex – particularly religious or ascetic persons, like clergymen or nuns. Although that at Borley Rectory did not seem dependant on any single person.

Two possible explanations are advanced for the association of phenomena with types of people. First, in the cases involving children trickery has been offered as the explanation, with a desire to increase self-importance as the motivating factor in the child.

In the cases involving adults the motivating factor for the trickery and deception, including self-deception, involved, is postulated to be the relief of severe internal conflicts caused by prolonged asceticism.

An example of the latter is given in the case of the Cure d'Ars (yes, unfortunately, that was his name) who was plagued by a very unpleasant poltergeist for 35 years. Nearly all its manifestations were witnessed by him alone, and amounted to a kind of persecution. The Cure, who died in 1859, was a renowned French priest, noted for his piety and an ability to achieve miraculous healings of some ailments. The malignant spirit which disturbed him caused noises, violent bed shakings, forcible levitations of his person, and the smearing of excrement on religious pictures – notably just before some afflicted person appealed to him for help. As the manifestations were not well-authenticated, it has been suggested that witnesses were unable to detect the trickery involved, "with all the cunning of which hysterics are capable," to fool them.

But not all poltergeists phenomena are explicable in terms of mere trickery.

A baffling case was described by Bishop Weston of Zanzibar in 1923. He reported that large clods of earth were violently detached from the walls of a native hut and hurled against the ceiling by some unseen force, even when the hut had been cleared, and a cordon of guards posted around it.

The famous haunting of Borley Rectory involved noises, temperature drops, locking of doors, messages scratched on walls, inexplicable lights, and other phenomena, for upwards of a century, before the place burnt down. It was investigated for fifteen years, without adequate explanation being found.

Even if the exaggeration, embroidery, practical jokes, and trickery, are accounted for, certain questions remain to be answered. The view of the professional investigator of the paranormal is that the poltergeist mechanism is similar to that of psychic mediumship – with the focal person as the medium.

In a standard work on, "Ghosts and Apparitions", W. H. Salter wrote: "There is a strong probability that any poltergeist worth investigating will be a product of subnormal adolescence." Writing in 1938 Salter added: "This was established half a century ago, and should now be common knowledge, and cases must be handled in such a way as to have regard for the child's mental and nervous welfare."

Salter seemed to assume that children are almost always the focus of psychokinetic (movement of objects without physical means) manifestations – but this is clearly not the case. What seems to be the regular feature in the agent is some kind of conflict, and a relative underdevelopment of control over unconscious mental functions – such as might be expected in children, and those devoted to religious practices, at the expense of their natural instincts. Rather than high intellect, low conscious development, and a relatively uninhibited, uncontrolled, manifestation of unconscious characteristics, in the person, is frequently apparent. This tends to suggest that rather than an advanced feature of human development, the affecting of objects by supernatural means is an archaic, and regressive feature, hearkening back to a primitive past.

Although clever, and almost convincing, explanations have been advanced for the phenomena of apparitions, few people are able to suggest anything beyond a vague connection with puberty for poltergeist disturbances. What triggers them, or how they happen, we simply do not know.

The coming of Christianity suppressed the European belief in innumerable spirits or supernatural beings, yet many survived in belief as demons, or evil spirits. Some were termed goblins, and could assume human shape, or that of animals and birds.

The Teutons of Northern Europe believed that the dead returned by night on the wings of wind and storm, as demonic spirits who tormented people in sleep. These nightriders were the originators of the term "nightmare".

Non-human demons, known as "elementals", lived in forests, on mountains, in lakes, streams, and wells, or crouched on men's' shoulders unseen, and brought them bad luck. Illness and insanity were explained as demonic possession.

Subsequent Christian views of demonology were influenced by the Hebrew tradition of the Old Testament. This originally had a limited concept of demons including Azazel, a demon of the wilderness, and Lilith, a female demon of the night associated with the moon, but it became elaborated through contact with Zoroastrian concepts of the spirit world to include the arch-demon Satan, with many lesser demons under his direction.

In China, the people were so afraid of the demons know as Kueis, which were thought to throng about everywhere at night, that they invented firecrackers to frighten them away, and built their houses with curving gables, so that they could not squat on the roof. The Chinese lantern was also intended to ward off demons, which the Chinese believed infested everything from water, soil, air, animals and plants, to mountains, forests, and inanimate objects.

But demons are not "just" poltergeists. At least that seems to be the lesson offered by the story I am about to relate. The story of a modern-day demon.

These experiences were witnessed by two highly intelligent young men whilst they were students on degree courses in London in the 1960s. The effect on at least one of them, whom I knew personally, was to convince him irrevocably of the real nature of the phenomena. And as it was a personal experience of this man, described in this own words, I do not give his name, but I have no reason to doubt his honesty.

One of the two young men, who shared a flat in South London, had acquired a curio in the form of a wooden charm. What he didn't know was that it was a bad luck charm. He described it thus: "The charm which attracted the demon was a black magic charm, made in the South

Sea, designed to bring ill-luck to its owner. It was about the size of a matchbox – a carving in very dark wood of a Polynesian or similar type face (stylized in the fashion of the Easter Island statues), with eyes of mother-of-pearl.

"Such a charm is 'magnetised' by a magician or magical group, and I was told by a very powerful clairvoyant and occultist we consulted, that the one I had, was magnetised with an artificial elemental, which in my case acted as a sort of magnet to the demon.

"The timescale of the developing attacks, from the time I acquired the charm, was about eighteen months in all. A bit longer if anything, certainly no less.

"The actual psychokinetic effects included a feeling of cold, a subtle alteration in the quality of the light, and awareness of the approaching presence of something extremely evil. I knew when it was coming, approximately how long it would take to get there, and from which physical direction it was approaching. While it was approaching I experienced a sense of terror and dread, which induced a kind of paralysis of thought and action. Above all, such things seem capable of putting fear and confusion into their victims. I speak, of course, as one who escaped ... thank God I do not know what sensations they engender in those they defeat."

South Sea mask of a malignant spirit known as Dogai and associated with "a bright star", in Cambridge University museum. It is similar in style to the demonic charm.

"The appearance of the demon ... A pulsating, translucent and only semi-visible entity a few feet in diameter. Globular in outline. Capable of "flying" – travelling through the air at will.

"Physical evidence of its effect on surrounding objects ... IT unlatched a gate, banging it against the direction of the wind. It also made fallen leaves swirl against the wind, as it moved along. At what it took to be the verge of its triumph (as far as I can gauge), it played on our fears, toying with us, in a grim humour. Remember the phrase; 'The banality of evil'.

"The means by which I escaped ... The help and support of a psychically aware friend, who was involved in the experience too. Help from the occultist already mentioned, my own psychological resources, such as they are, and – in the final analysis – prayer; by which I mean throwing myself on the mercy of the powers of light and asking for their help. I prayed to God, using a particular name for Him as advised by the occultist.

"At the time of the destruction of the charm by burning, it failed to alight for many minutes, but shrank until quite small. Only then did it burn as such. The light in the room throughout the episode – not just when it caught fire – took on a nasty yellow tinge. When my friend went to flush the ash down the loo, he received an electrical-type shock, and was thrown against a wall.

"Before the attacks began, I had experienced developing psychism, especially precognitions. I also had feeling of hopelessness, disorientation, purposelessness, and stultification of thought processes. There were also feelings of existential terror – 'the gaps between the stars are so much more vast than the stars.' And a lot of incidents I put down to bad luck."

"When the attacks were over I felt blessed relief, joy, delight. I was aware of having a very narrow shave. I took great pleasure at what I had learned – that there is an existence beyond the physical, and an after-life, but above all that the supreme power in the universe is good and will help people, however insignificant they may be, if they are in the type of fix I was. Really it was the most significant experience, or series of experiences, in my life, and it led to a sort of intellectual revolution in me. Not that I had any illusions about being holier-than-thou, or holier than anybody after the attacks, and events subsequently proved that I could still be quite capable of misjudgements – but I did feel, and still do, spiritually liberated, if you see what I mean. It was much too massive an experience, and too complicated to put down in much less than a book, if I was telling the whole tale."

My friend was never bothered by the demon again, although not long afterwards he was involved in a serious road accident, which took him a long time to recover from. Sometime before this, he also had the misfortune to fall between the platform and a stationary tube train in a London Underground station, and was only rescued by the quick action of a fellow passenger. He partly attributes the influence of the demonic karma to both incidents. But as he says, he was very lucky to escape alive in either case.

As an amusing postscript it is worth mentioning that during the demonic attacks, whilst frantically searching for knowledge with which to ward off the evil, my friend visited a well-known occult bookshop in London. The staff were intrigued by his problem. "They said some of their customers had been hoping all their lives to contact a demon and here was I – successful, and all I wanted was to get rid of it!" However, they directed him to a book on psychic self-defence which did the trick. Sadly my friend developed heart trouble, whilst still a young man, and died despite extensive surgery.

8

MYSTERIOUS MEGALITHS

"I could feel the specific moods of old objects in particular, and it was in this state that I encountered either accidentally, or through the intervention of higher – I hope higher – forces, an ancient monument. Through this monument, which I accidentally tapped, by the use of certain active substances in collaboration with a few words of antiquity, I learned the secret of relation of the two great cosmic laws."

These startling words are attributed to the occult philosopher, Georgei Ivanovitch Gurdjieff, delivered by him to a select and secret group of his pupils, who consider themselves to be in possession of knowledge which heralds the coming of a new age. He continued:

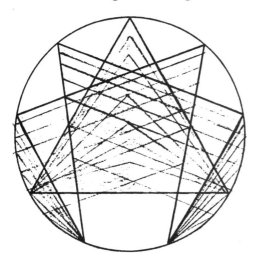

The enneagram – a representation of the living world.

"The emotional impact of receiving data from objects which were in themselves sentient beings was enormous on my own presence. It was as if I had never existed except to perceive and appreciate, in their absolute states, everything about them."

"I saw also, through the medium of this giant dolmen, a geometric form deep within it, which formed a sphere with nine planes intersecting at intervals. These planes continually folded in on each other, and on themselves, creating the effect of a lotus collapsing inward upon itself. I understood at once that this was the form of the living world, and that should I somehow prematurely penetrate beyond this formation, it would cause my annihilation just as surely as would absorption into infinity."

Giant dolmens, stone circles, mysterious megaliths – why did an ancient culture, who had only managed to fashion the stone axe, and spearhead, devote so much time, effort, and sheer muscle power, to hewing and shifting enormous blocks of stone, and levering them into difficult positions, on hills, and in valleys?

There have been many far-fetched answers, and archaeologists do not help by merely stating the obvious – or what they think is the obvious. I have in mind the observations, of a Victorian archaeologist, that the explanation of burial chambers, and mounds was quite simple. In days before metal tools, such as spades were invented, it was much easier to dispose of the dead by heaping rubble, or enormous megalithic monuments over them, than by digging! Having observed the size of some of the rocks involved, I think he may have been a little off the mark.

Alfred Watkins, with his book, "The Old Straight Track" began a positive sub science of speculation with his theory of ley lines, which were supposed to use ancient monuments as sighting points to enable prehistoric man to navigate his way across trackless land.

"Imagine a fairy chain stretched from mountain peak to mountain peak, as far as the eye could reach, and paid out until it touched the high places of the earth at a number of ridges, banks and knolls. Then visualise a mound, circular earthwork or clump of trees, planted on these high points, and, in low points in the valley, other mounds, ringed with water, to be seen from a distance. Then great standing stones, brought to mark the way at intervals … " Alfred Watkins was a Hereford businessman and antiquary, who made his discovery by chance observation of alignments. Many subsequent writers have taken his theories much further, and suggest that ley lines may be a channel for mysterious energy.

The only problem with the idea of leys as a guidance system for travellers is the difficulty of constantly marching over the highest points of hills and ridges, as any experienced walker would testify, there are easier ways to traverse country. Also, in prehistoric times, the much thicker forest land would have obscured many of the supposed marker points which are visible in our barer landscape today.

The ley hunter's favourite pastime is examining maps, with clear plastic rulers, to see how many "leys" can be discovered by joining such diverse objects in a straight line as cairns, churches, standing stones, hill tops, ancient monuments and so on. It would be an unresourceful ley hunter who could not discover at least one such, to satisfy his curiosity, on any map, as you only require a minimum of three features to qualify as a "ley".

As for the transmission of mysterious energy – what was it for, and how did it get from one megalithic monument to another? One suggestion is that leys were somehow ground beacons, or guidance paths for flying saucers. However, we first have to consider the case for both flying saucers, and mysterious energy transmission adequately· made out, before contemplating that one.

Supposing we accept, or postulate, the idea that there is some form of residual energy, currently unknown to modern science, associated with megalithic sites. It still does not make any sense to suppose that one site is somehow connected by invisible power lines to another. The more sceptical reader may object that it is just as illogical to accept that any energy resides in a jumble of lifeless rocks, so why not go the whole hog, and embrace ley lines too!

People are very suggestible, but very many different types of person have testified to odd experiences at megalithic monuments. Gifted dowsers, who can find both hidden streams and buried metal as proof of their craft, are strongly affected by some of the stones on ancient sites. Some even claim to have received electric type shocks! Photographs of the heat sensitive variety have turned out to show rays of light exuding from the monoliths.

Recent research with magnetometers discovered the existence of concentric rings of electromagnetic force within the Rollright stone circle in Oxfordshire. This circle was examined minutely over a prolonged period, and produced a variety of inexplicable phenomena.

The stones sang, for instance – that is, exactly an hour before dawn in the period immediately preceding the Spring and Autumn equinox, the stones began to emit ultrasonic bleeps, before elapsing into silence again. Sudden, and unaccountable bursts of radioactivity proceeded from a monolith in the centre of the circle, and a general impression of some kind of energy activity, registered by instruments, was proven to exist here.

Again, a variety of speculative "explanations" have been put forward
– including what must be the prize – that megalithic monuments of this
kind were intended as radioactive fall-out shelters!

In order to put the megaliths into perspective, perhaps we should
examine their "known" history. It is a fondness of academics to treat
that which is written in the proverbial text-book as irrefutable fact,
when, in "fact", that which is "known" originated as speculation in its
day, and was "proved" by a methodology based on accepted assump-
tions.

Take the assumption of the fail-safe dating by carbon 14. This is as
"certain" as our knowledge of the ages of the dinosaurs, and the extent
of the geological epochs, where, between Paleozoic and Mesozoic we
can "give or take" a few million years. I may not be a scientist, but I ask
the simple question – how do we know that the radioactive half-life of
carbon 14 (its rate of radioactive decomposition) never changes. Who has
been alive for the thousands of years required to check? The scientist
may smile a condescending smile and say: "Well in the laboratory we do
a little test, and we estimate ... " Yes! You estimate. You cannot prove.
In fact most of science is an assumption based on the known data which
more or less fits, is more or less to the purpose.

But scientific results can be adjusted to ignore contradictions, and
thereby ignore the inconsistencies in creation. And the wider and more
arty the subject, the greater the inconsistencies. Take archaeology.

According to the evidence, what is termed the Neolithic, or New
Stone Age, from about 3,000 or 1,900 BC, was the period in which the
megaliths were erected. Remember that these Herculean tasks were all
performed by a people who left no trace of their actual living communities in the form of their dwellings, or any vestige other than stone tools,
and weapons, earthenware beakers and jars, and incredibly enduring
stone monuments, devoted largely, according to archaeologists, as
sepulchres to the dead.

This seems an inordinately fruitless object of such mammoth efforts
by small pastoral communities. We know nothing of their religion or
cosmological beliefs, but archaeological evidence indicates that they were
a simple farming people, who had developed improved methods of
making stone tools, and had skills in pottery.

The importance of knowing the seasons for planting, and animal
husbandry, had been advanced as one reason why some stone circles
have been identified as vast astronomical clocks, capable of being used

in calculating the movements of the sun, moon, and stars, during the year, as a kind of astral calendar. The circles are not always perfect in shape, and can be flattened or oval in outline, but it has been suggested that these "primitive" people must have had some mathematical knowledge to construct them so accurately, in relation to heavenly bodies.

Apart from solitary standing stones, or menhirs, the most common form of megalithic monuments are the barrows, cromlechs, dolmens or burial chambers. Whether we believe that these were merely archaic edifices, for disencumbering the living of the dead, or whether something more involved was believed to be the case by the people who expended so much effort in building them, they remain unique in the history of architecture, even if the beliefs which inspired them are forgotten.

Professor Alexander Thom has made calculations which show the circles he examined were constructed with incredible accuracy. Many burial mounds involved the levering into place of enormous capstones resting on stone uprights. These stone tables, frequently denuded of their original covering of earth and stones, were named dolmen from the Breton tol (table) and men (stone) by a French archaeologist in 1796.

The tables, also known as cromlechs from the Welsh crwm (curved) and llech (stone), are thought sometimes to have never been covered with mounds, but remained free-standing! They were often used for subsequent purposes by later cultures, and are associated with superstitious legends even today. The Druids utilised them as altars, in their rites, but the megaliths are the product of a far earlier people than the Celts. Such monuments are spread all over Europe, and other parts of the world – Gurdjieff found some in the Caucausus mountains of Central Asia. Around the Western fringes of Britain they seem to have been largely the work of a sea-borne people, possibly Iberian in origin, and definitely a Mediterranean culture.

Why they came, and why they built such lasting memorials we don't know. There are theories that they were, "following the sun", and that this embodied part of their religious quest. Cromlechs and barrows are usually aligned East-West, facing the rising, and setting suns. Archaeology is just as much 'in the dark' over stone circles. Sir Mortimer Wheeler speculated that: "It is likely enough that some of the stone circles were like medieval churches, used for communal, secular, no less than for religious purposes, in an age when the two were essentially one, and indivisible." But many archaeologists do not claim to know the answer.

Among the impressive cromlechs of Wales is that of Pentre Ifan, near Newport, Dyfed. It is 16.5ft long, balanced 7.5ft above the ground on three tapering upright stones, giving an impression of lightness, and strength. All the stones in this chamber were quarried and brought from the Preseli Hills – which also provided the famous bluestones of Stonehenge. What was so important about this type of stone, that it was transported so far? Transport in those days was a very laborious process of hauling on rollers of logs, which had to be continually renewed in front of the moving object. Was there some special property of this type of stone, more to the purpose of the megalith builders, that it was transported so far?

Pentre Ifan
Steve Cliffe

Pentre Ifan, the largest dolmen in Wales, near Newport.

Let us take the example of a minor stone circle – the Druids Circle, 2 miles south of Penmaenmawr, in North Wales, and examine the legends attached to it. One stone in the circle is known as the Deity Stone, and it is believed that if anyone used bad language near it, the stone would tilt over and hit the offensive person. The Stone of Sacrifice has a cavity on top, large enough to hold a small child. It was once believed that if anyone put a baby there in the first months of its life it would always be lucky. Yet horrible cries are thought to proceed from this stone on stormy nights. Witches holding a meeting outside the circle were once terrified when a stern warning was issued from the stone. It is said that the effect was so sudden that one woman died on the spot, and another went raving mad.

These legends – of talking stones, walking stones, spinning stones, and stones that go for a drink, or even swim, were often associated with miraculous healings and fertility.

There were two lesser circles, or three, or four, thought to be to the West of the one mentioned above, which is in a bleak and lonely spot, atop a mountain above Conwy Bay. In one of these, since demolished, were said to be three coloured stones, each denoting the colour of dress of three women, turned to stone there for working on a Sunday. This myth of women turned to stone for dancing, working etc., is a very common one, and will merit sociological explanation by competent feminists.

A woman friend pointed out the curiously genitalian formation of a burial chamber dating from 2,500 – 1,900 BC at Capel Garmon, in North Wales. There are two circular burial chambers – one to the East, and one to the West, with an entrance passage from the South. When viewed from above, and in outline on plans, the monument gives the appearance of male reproductive organs, with the southerly entrance passage as the phallus. She suggested that the reason for this was that the whole structure was regarded as a life regeneration system by its builders!

The same woman and I had a curious experience while visiting the famous Bryn Celli Ddu burial chamber on Anglesey, one Autumn dusk as a full moon rose above the trees. This is one of the few dolmen still covered by a mound of earth. It is also within a stone circle which pre-dates the chamber itself, indicating a clash of religious cultures, archaeologists believe.

It is approached down a long farm-track and can be seen across undulating fields for some distance. A stone upright with incised patterns stands by the entrance portal and a rusty iron gate leads into a narrow passage, causing visitors to stoop, brushing their shoulders on either side, as they enter the central chamber. This is roofed by a huge flat capstone, or rather two, as there is a major split, just off-centre. Light is admitted via the Western facing hatch, or portal, blocked by a boulder reaching to chest height.

Bryn Celli Ddu – does it contain sentient energy?

To one side of the chamber is a curious rounded pillar, unusual in megalithic monuments, smooth and with no visible incised patterns on it. Said to be over eight feet in height, it stops short of the roof by several inches.

During our hurried visit, I asked the lady to feel the pillar and see if any impressions could be obtained. She said nothing, but left the chamber hurriedly after touching the pillar for a minute or so.

Outside, it was getting dark and she was clearly distressed. As we walked back along the track she began to speak haltingly of the impression from the pillar. She said that it seemed to her to be violently aggressive. She had never received an impression like it elsewhere. "It seemed to be thrusting up into my chest," she almost sobbed. "I felt I had to get out."

Thus it might have ended, but in the following weeks I saw my friend again. "I have been dreaming of it," she told me. "It seems to want me." In her dream the woman saw the pillar, charged with menace, brooding and assertive. It *had* patterns on it. Chevrons, or wavy lines, covered the pillar and she knew in the dream that they were painted – in blood!

Turning to the known archaeological evidence on the monument we were both surprised and a little chilled to read: "When it was excavated large quantities of both burned and unburned human bones were found. It may once have been a site of human sacrifice as well as a burial chamber."

An acquaintance who knows something of the symbols used in witchcraft told us, "the chevron, depending on whether it is facing up or down, denotes war." It also has Druidical associations.

We know little more than this, but my friend retains a horror of the site to this day.

The Isle of Man, for such a small island, is particularly rich in Neolithic monuments, so much so, that one might speculate as to the necessity of such splendid tombs for the limited number of inhabitants. Perhaps, as in Iona, after the coming of Christianity, chiefs and noted men were brought here, from across the seas, to this hallowed land for burial – if from the mainland, it would be towards the setting sun.

Cashtal Yn Ard is a massive burial chamber, with a semi-circular forecourt in the West. Here unburnt human bones, pottery and flints were found. To the East is a mound of earth and stones reddened and fused by heat. The entire monument, which contains five separate stone chambers was once covered by a massive cairn of earth and stones 130ft long.

King Orry's Grave, at Lonan, is a similar structure, only this also has a U-shaped forecourt in the East giving access to the chamber. The unexcavated West appears to have had another forecourt, with access to a separate chamber of two compartments divided by a miniature portal.

A hauntingly fascinating circle of burial cists, of unique design, the Meayll, lies on a hillside, overlooking the sea near Port Erin. There are six pairs of T-shaped chambers, with the head of the T facing into the circle, and the trunk of the T as the entrance passage. In the centre of the circle, when I visited it, was a large piece of quartz – a white crystalline stone, often associated with these sites. More interesting perhaps, was the fact that the Eastern and Western gates into the circle align, across this stone, with two naturally-occurring veins of quartz, in rock outcrops to the East and West of the circle. This suggests, to me, at least, that the circle had been deliberately situated in this position, in alignment with

the quartz veins, for some purpose of which we are ignorant. All I can add, is that quartz is often regarded to have a symbolic (?) association with the substance of spirit.

All these monuments were constructed in about 2,000 BC. An older one on the island, dating from 3,000 – 2,500 BC remains at Ballakelly. It consists of a horseshoe arrangement of stone uprights around a single burial chamber. A pattern of rows of "cup mark" type rings decorate a stone behind the burial chamber. Patterned decoration of megalithic tombs is fairly rare, and the marks, made laboriously with stone on stone, must have had a special significance.

The Meayl stone circle and its burial cists. Phantom horsemen are reported nearby.

Two burial chambers on Anglesey have stones with designs cut into them, but most decoration of this kind is found in Ireland. In one of these two, Barclodiad-y-Gawres, situated on a dramatic headland on the rocky West coast of the island near Rhosneigr, archaeologists found a strange collection of burnt remains in the centre of the tomb. Beneath the silent stones, with their mysterious spiral and zig zag (chevron) patterns, were remains of pigs vertebrae, whiting, eels, a frog, a toad, a snake, a mouse, a shrew, and a hare – apparently the recipe of some former witches' brew, and probably not contemporary with the monument. At the other patterned Anglesey chamber, Bryn Celli Ddu, were unusually large quantities of burned and unburned human bones. Here, it is thought human sacrifice may have taken place, in later ages than those of the megalith builders.

So how crazy is Gurdjieff's idea that such monuments could be ancient repositories of knowledge? The strange patterns of rings, zig zags, and spirals must have had a meaning to their inscribers – but more likely they also had a purpose, like the hieroglyphs on Egyptian tombs, which were to aid the dead in their quest to the underworld, and rebirth. The idea that inert rocks could be "charged" with knowledge may have seemed absurd – until the silicon chip was invented. Most rocks are composed chiefly of silicon, which, after carbon, the basic element of biological structures, including man, is the most plentiful element on earth. In fact it has been postulated that if life had not evolved around structures based on the carbon atom, it could have done so around silicon ...

What "matter" is the vehicle for the spirit of life? The thought gives an entirely new perspective to the phrase, "spirit which dwelt in a house of clay". For those who regard the psyche as a product of the brain, this is all nonsense, but I will deal more fully with these ideas in the final chapter ...

Instead, take the example of an incident which happened in the vicinity of a little-known, and ancient cromlech, situated in the Conwy Valley of North Wales, as told by a friend:

"A famous survival expert and SAS instructor once described in some detail how he avoided the belligerent attentions of a single bull whilst crossing a field. This involved his dropping a back-pack to distract and delay the animal, while he made for an adjacent tree, in which he was obliged to reside for a full hour, until it had gored his pack, and the contents to shreds. My wife and I had to contend with not one (we should have been so lucky) but upwards of a hundred mixed bulls and heifers in a very frisky mood."

"My previous experience of bulls; and I have lived on a farm; was that although they will frequently charge, sometimes in a body, when your back is turned, they are usually discouraged by a loud yell and the brandishing of a stick."

"On this occasion, we had decided to walk over some farm-land to visit the site of the old cromlech before it went dark. The journey involved a vigorous climb over gates, and through hedges, skirting woods and stream-beds, to get to where the cromlech; half in, and half out of a fence between two fields; nestled among some trees, overlooking the broad and winding estuary of the River Conwy."

"It was late June, with a clear sky. A new crescent moon had risen in the East, and the blood-red streaks of a dying sun sank over the dark mountainous bulk of the Western horizon, on the other side of the valley. It was already going dusk as we entered a field full of cattle, some of which, disturbed in their evening ponderings, began to drift towards us."

"By the next field, the drift had become a stampede. It was clear that we should have to make it to the trees, beyond which lay the cromlech, in double quick time. Shouts and arm waving only seemed to alert more cattle to the fun, and the entire herd began a downhill sweep in our direction. "Run", I said, and we did, putting the first trees between us and the leading cattle just in time to slow their rush to a trot."

"They did not give up however. In among the trees they darted. My wife had disappeared up the banking in the direction of the fence, and I found myself confronted on three sides by beasts making little rushes every time my back was turned. Footholds were uncertain on the rough ground, and I was trying to use one tree to avoid all three. Fortunately I found a stick, and the next sally was met by a blow on the nose. That dissuaded one animal, and as the others paused, I rushed for the fence. As I did so, out of the corner of my eye I saw another bull literally charging through the trees downhill – and directly in its path was my wife. I opened my mouth to shout, but before I did so, she uttered the most horrendous shout of belligerence I have heard from a woman. The bull, hurtling downhill as it was, applied all brakes, its hooves scouring the earth, skidding to a halt, and enveloping the surrounding wood in a cloud of dust and stones."

"More cattle were coming, and I dashed with her for the megalith, lying darkly between the fence. It was high, but I was at it with one bound, ignoring the tearing sound from my trouser seams. By the time I gained the megalith, twenty cattle were at the fence, pushing and jostling, their muzzles straining over. Behind them came scores more, weaving through the trees, and obviously in a bullying mood. My wife appeared to be wavering on the fence, higher up the field, attended by several bovine admirers. She seemed uncertain as to my predicament, and in two minds whether to climb back over and distract them. "Get over the fence," I yelled. And she did so, walking down on the bull-free side towards me with a wry grin."

"She sat down on the grass, and I, on top of the megalith, and she on the ground, exchanged anecdotes of our respective adventures. The cattle meanwhile continued to lean and shove against the fence, straining and tossing their heads, while others, rearing up, began to do to the heifers, what bulls do, in their close proximity."

"I surveyed the herd. Its outriders and stragglers had all come in, attracted by the spectacle. A heaving mass of brown bodies, heads and horns, tightly packed bull-flesh, jostled and bullied at the foot of the ancient monument, atop which, like a bard of old, stood I, balefully regarded by many pairs of great brown bovine eyes."

"Trying to look into them for any expression of significance, all I could discern was herd instinct, and dumb, uncritical, curiosity."

"I recited a few poems to them, with impressive gestures, but it didn't seem to have much effect. They just went on staring, jostling, stamping and pushing. As I looked, I gained a remarkable insight into the nature of the star-sign Taurus."

"This caused me to remember the megalith, and reflect that, as it was so seldom visited with such an adequate guard of honour to attend it on one side, and the river on the other, perhaps it might contain an interesting residue of impressions."

"This cromlech is on private land, and although marked on the O.S. map, is not easy to get to. It is, however, very impressive, having a massive capstone between three and four feet thick, and supported on heavy stone uprights, some of which have collapsed. In the West, facing the dying sun, is a large entrance, and judging by the fleece scourings, and droppings inside, it is often a sheltering place for sheep."

"According to local historians it is known as Allor Molloch – the altar of Molloch. Who Molloch was I don't know, but as the name implies that the cromlech was used for religious rites, it seems reasonable to presume that he may have been a Druid. As far as is known, the Iberian people who built the cromlechs did not use them as altars, but who knows what practices their burial rites entailed? However the Druids are thought to have frequently purloined megaliths as suitable venues for their rituals. Gurdjieff had some interesting ideas about utilising the stray energies, residual in ancient monuments, connected with extinct religious practices – including old priories."

"Rene Guenon, mentioning the ancient practice of shamanism, on which most pagan belief systems seem to have been based, remarks that it is known, in connection with what is termed "sacred geography" that sanctuaries, shrines, and places of pilgrimage serve as repositories of spiritual and benefic psychic influences, and that:

"There are in the world a certain number of reservoirs of influences, the distribution of which is certainly no matter of chance"

"One ancient monument, having been charged with energy under ancient rites, seems as good as another according to this theory."

"Anyway, as I stood atop Allor Molloch, I did what I should have learned not to do in places of past or present psychic activity. I cleared my mind, ignoring the cattle, which were now more interested in one another, than us. I began a system of meditation breathing, to help prevent normal thoughts and associations recurring, and blocking the impressions which I sought from the megalith."

"I was facing the crescent moon, which was fast rising over the south eastern hills, and there was complete stillness, on a warm evening, with not a breath of wind. Suddenly, I felt as if my entire left arm, from the shoulder to hand, had been enveloped in a deep-freeze cold. It happened so suddenly there was no question of a shiver. My hand began to tingle in the palm, and continued to do so even after I climbed down off the cromlech. When my wife felt the palm, she also could feel a slight tingling, like an electrical pulse. The coldness went as suddenly as it had come, but the tingling lingered. It became clear to me later, from the experiences of other people during psychic happenings, that the cold denotes an energy drain taking place, and the tingling, in my case, seemed to be the after-effect of its cessation."

"Lethbridge mentions this phenomena in his book, *A step in the Dark.* I did not see or hear anything. But later, as I crouched by the Western entrance portal to the tomb, and looked towards the gloaming of the hidden sun, a hypnogogic vision of a typical interlaced Celtic pattern

A weird stone and bush in Northern Anglesey. Glacial deposits like this were frequently used as capstones for Cromlechs.

flashed momentarily before my eyes, so quickly I could not recall its exact form. This may have been the effect of suggestion on the unconscious mind, but I am inclined to believe that something resides in the cromlech, about which we know nothing at all, with some polarity of its own, and having a capacity fo flow, like current, into, or away from, a suitable source."

This is the most extensive account of 'tapping' a megalith I have recorded.

The element of regeneration, or rebirth, is quite clear at a number of well-known megalithic structures. At Newgrange in Ireland, the impressive tomb, with its 20ft high corbelled ceiling, has a slit over the entrance which permits the sun, dawning on a clear midwinters day, to penetrate 62ft down the central passage, illuminating the burial chamber. The whole structure of Newgrange seems to have been orientated towards midwinter, and a theme of rebirth and renewal.

Situated above a bend in the River Boyne, the entire burial mound originally had a covering of white quartz stones, so that, surrounded by its silent sentinels of standing stones, it would have appeared like a dazzling white cone above the river. An array of spiral and zig zag patterns here have baffled archaeologists. This very elaborate tomb was constructed as long ago as 3,300 BC – at a time before the Egyptian pyramids were built. White quartz, or sand, is still scattered in Irish graves during burial.

At Ballochroy, on the west coast of Scotland, another megalithic tomb has been so constructed that an alignment of three nearby stones point to the setting of the sun at midwinter. Another example.

What is even odder are a series of illustrations of concentric circles, made on rocks in Northumberland. They bear a striking resemblance to the appearance of a single sperm cell, as it approaches and breaches the female egg, in the act of fertilization, as viewed through a powerful microscope! These designs were first noted in 1860 – before the science of genetics was even developed.

Spirals on rock, not far from the stone circle and cairn cemetery at Cauldside Burn, Kirkcudbright, Scotland, are represented as a kind of maze, with a passage offering a return from the innermost spiral, all the way back to the outer.

I may be completely wrong, but it seems to me, from the evidence of sun, moon, and star watching by these ancients; the mammoth task of erecting tombs; their preoccupation with the upward swing of the sun at midwinter – that these were motifs of rebirth, describing the descent of the soul from the outer to the inner, and its return, in a never-ending spiral of existence.

Whether the Neolithic people believed in an actual physical rebirth – perhaps into the tribe, is another question. Possibly their idea was that the souls of the dead lived on, regenerated by these tombs, in situ, looking over the fortunes of the tribe who honoured them. Or perhaps the souls of the dead were thought to escape, through the western portal, following the immortal path – into a land of golden splendour – a blood red land of the dying sun.

9

GHOSTLY MISCELLANY

What follows should be an interesting series of ghostly stories, hardly any of which have ever been heard before. In almost any corner of the far flung globe, if one were to enquire diligently among the natives, primitive or otherwise, I am sure a similar series of entertaining and inexplicable tales could be found. But what is land without its folklore – nothing but barren rock and earth, impersonal and dead. Populate it with mysteries and heroes from the past, and it comes alive in the imagination – adding an extra dimension to life itself.

As the majority of material in this books arises out of my own personal experience of the supernatural, certain areas tend to crop up regularly – despite this, they can be taken as legitimate examples of the type of phenomena, sociological, or psychic, which can appear anywhere in the world. Geographically speaking, my own travels have been frequently confined to parts of the North of England.

I am very familiar with a certain hill, one of the first rolling green buttresses of the Western Pennines, which rises out of the sprawling urban mass of the Greater Manchester conurbation like a stranded whale – above the mills, housing estates, motorways and blocks of flats spewing over the lowlands. It is a vital fresh green lung for the weary town dweller, and, in fact, has recently been designated a country park – the destination of many a car-load of trippers.

As one of the foremost flanks of the Pennines, with a fine view over the plain – as far as the Welsh mountains on a clear day, Werneth Low, is naturally beloved of those who appreciate commanding positions. People liked it in the Bronze Age – several burial mounds were constructed here, with fine views of the setting sun. On the Westernmost ridge of Werneth Low there is a striking view in almost every direction. Here the hill seems to end abruptly in space with far horizons, and on a clear night its trajectory is aimed at the stars. Here also perches an ancient stone farmhouse, around which the wind never ceases to moan.

Werneth Low – a hill held sacred by the Druids?

A story is told of a farmer who lived at Lowtop in the sixties. He was not a native of the area, and shortly after he came to the farm he was ploughing some fields near an exposed plantation of trees. As he did so, he gradually became aware of an impression of a figure dressed in white, standing at the edge of the wood, and watching him. Later, when out riding with his daughter, they both had the same impression again; that at a corner of this lower field, a white-robed figure was standing on the edge of the plantation, simply watching them, in a baleful way. On this occasion, as they rode close to the wood, the horses became agitated, finally, hysterical, and refused to pass the spot where the figure had been seen. The farmer, who was a Scot by birth, said the figure looked like a Druid.

What he only learned later was that close by this wood are several Bronze Age burial mounds, which were broken open and robbed of their stones by a much earlier farmer in the 18th century. The then president of the Lancashire and Cheshire Antiquarian Society recorded that: "Before the mounds could be examined, a local peasant, of the name of Bagshaw, carted the stone away to repair buildings, and make gateposts." Was the farmer of Lowtop an innocent recipient of the Druid's wrath?

The wood near which the Druid was seen is called Springwood – because a spring perpetually runs here, filling an old stone water-trough, and providing drinking water at another farm, lower down the hill. Springs were often the seat of Celtic shrines, sacred to the Druids.

The haunted trackway on Werneth Low

On another part of Werneth Low is a very muddy and rock-strewn gully or track, known by the locals as London Road. Now little more than a stream-bed, and made almost impassable by overhanging holly bushes, it is supposed to be haunted by a phantom charioteer – possibly Roman. Certainly no-one could get a chariot down there nowadays. But a number of people who live nearby have heard the sound of jingling harness without seeing anything. A new occupant at Needhams Farm, higher up the hill, commented on it, as did an old man, who lived in a wooden bungalow nearby. I know a man who lived in a caravan almost next to the gully who also heard something strange.

He was awakened one night in the small hours by the sound of a horse being led down the gully. He knows it was being led, because it was "stepping short". When the noise reached a large oak tree, which marks the end of the gully, and its junction with a farm-track, it paused, and then passed on, by the caravan, and up towards the nearby farm. Not very strange, until one considers that although my friend looked out onto the road, nothing could be seen, and the track leading up to the farm is a dead end – unless you go on up the hill, back into the gully!

"It was a funny time of night to be leading a horse," was my friend's comment. He suggested that perhaps the owner had been "walking off" an attack of equestrian colic. There were no reports of horses stolen on this very dark and windy night. However it was made more memorable for my friend, because his favourite black cat went out, and never came back, nor did he ever discover what happened to it.

My wife and I have both heard an inexplicable jingling noise near this caravan at night. Once, it was close to the gully, when there were no animals in the adjacent fields. Another time we heard it much nearer, and more clearly, in fields below the cricket club, one moonlit, frosty night. It sounded like someone shaking a chain – a sort of metallic chinking noise, which seemed to move across the field behind some wooden bungalows which obstructed our view. We heard it twice, then it ceased, but when we gained higher ground there was no-one about, and no horses or other animals in the field to account for it. On each occasion we heard the noises when thinking of things far removed from anything supernatural. Archaeologists have since confirmed that the gully is the site of a Roman road.

An interesting story of a corpse candle, or something like it, originated from this area, and gained general currency in ghostlore. It concerned an ancient farming family named Tym, one of the daughters of whom was tending an ailing relative. However, as the invalid had improved, she chanced a visit to friends in nearby Gee Cross. Returning across the fields however, she was frightened by the sudden and violent agitation of a hawthorn hedge on a windless day, and approaching the farm-house, she saw a light, or candle, pass from the door, and across the fields. When she got in, the patient was dead.

Perhaps it is fitting to conclude this series of corpse candles, jinglings of ancient Celtic horse goddesses, and dispossessed Druids, by describing another "mystery" of Werneth Low.

A farmer at Far Cloughside was startled one morning by inexplicable marks in his slurry pit, as if some large creature had been moving about in it, finally leaving a trail of slime through the farmyard and along the track towards Compstall village. The mystery remained until he met the wife of a notorious "tippler" nearby. Apparently her nearest and dearest had undergone an unwarranted ordeal. While returning from a hilltop hostelry known then and now as the "Hare and Hounds", he had got lost in the fields, stumbling into the cowshed at Far Cloughside, and plunged inadvertently into the slurry pit, where he spent nearly two hours, in the middle of the night, trying to get out.

He was so exhausted when he eventually staggered home, caked in pungent slime from head to foot, that he climbed into bed, clothes, manure, and all, pulled the quilt over him and went to sleep. What his wife said in the morning we are left to guess!

From the North, we go to the South of England, and the story of a kindly ghost told me by a descendant of the people involved. The Coles were a family of Quakers, who lived near Sevenoaks in Kent. They were respectable and no-nonsense business people in the 19th century, and the great, great, grandfather of the gentleman who told me this story had just been to the funeral of his widowed sister, who lived at Tenterden. He had decided to assume responsibility for the two orphaned children of his sister, and was returning from the funeral to Sevenoaks, with them, in an open horse-drawn trap, when he noticed the figure of a woman in the road. Drawing nearer, he realised with a shock that it was his sister, in her normal everyday clothes, and she was holding up her hands and gesticulating frantically to him. As he had just buried her, Mr Cole was a little disturbed by the apparition, which, as the trap drew near, rushed forward and seemed to grasp the reins of the horses, which came to an abrupt halt. No sooner had they done so, than an enormous oak tree fell with a sickening crash across the road in front.

There was never any doubt in his mind that had the trap not been stopped both he, and the children, would have been killed, and although he lived to be nearly a hundred, he always maintained that he had seen his sister, a few hours after her funeral, dressed normally as he saw her in life, and that she had saved his life, and that of her children.

Another ghost associated with families is the banshee of Ireland. Traditionally they are heard rather than seen, and are said to exude howls and wails from the bottom of wells at the approaching death of a member of family. When seen, their hair is said to be tangled, like seaweed.

This story concerns the sighting of a banshee, described as an enormous woman, at Eglington in Northern Ireland. A member of the Gallaher family was dying, and the grandmother of the person who told me this story was staying at the small farmhouse, while her own mother tended the sick man. As she was a young girl, she had been sent upstairs to bed and told that if she heard anything in the night to stay put. Meanwhile her mother and other relatives tended the old man, who was lying in a box bed, near the kitchen fire downstairs. He was 94, and had been a farmer all his life, noted for his energy and vigour. Because it was a warm summer night, the door to the farmyard had been left open. The women had just looked at the dying man. It was about 4 a.m. and beginning to come light outside.

"My great grandmother happened to look to the door, and saw the figure of a very tall woman, silhouetted, in the morning light, in the door-frame. As she looked, the stranger let out an unearthly cry, like a goat being killed – not like the cry of a human voice. Then the figure ran across the farmyard, and jumped onto a low wall, running along the top, still uttering the unearthly shriek, and distractedly pulling at her hair. Finally, she leap down, and disappeared."

The women were too stunned to follow, and when they looked at the old man, he was, of course, dead. Possibly from shock?

Meanwhile, my friend's grandmother was upstairs, quivering under the bedclothes, but staying put. The Gallaher family was known to have a banshee, and the figure had been expected to appear, but the great grandmother had never seen the figure before, and she never saw it again, even though she was at the deathbed of other members of the family. No explanation was ever forthcoming.

The banshee was described as having a frenzied, demented appearance, with tangled hair. The family were fervently religious protestants, passionate, imaginative, demonstrative, and fond of theatre.

This story is about a little boy, who lived in an Edwardian semi – like millions of other respectable Accrington brick villas which dot suburbia, unexciting and unremarkable. This one was slightly different in that it had been built, and lived in, by a funeral director, who used the rear outhouse as a chapel of rest. Even the laying out board still remained as a grisly reminder of the former occupant's vocation. It was a dark and dreary house. All the windows seemed to face away from the sun – possibly they had been designed this way. Only the setting sun of the evening penetrated the gloomy interior, and on the hottest summer day, it was as cold as the tomb. I know because I once lived there.

The little boy was poorly with measles at the time of his experience, and was sleeping in the downstairs back sitting room, beneath a fanlight in a bay window, which sometimes admitted a shaft of moonlight onto a mandala-like pattern, in a blue Indian carpet near the bed. One night the child thought he'd woken up, and looking round, saw the figure of a man, and a small girl, of about eight, in Edwardian dress, standing on the Indian carpet. He was a tall thin man wearing a black frock coat. The girl had her back to the boy, and he noticed her long well-brushed fair hair. The two appeared to be having a conversation, and the little girl slightly obscured the boy's view of the man. Then she stepped aside, and he could see the man's hands, which were trembling and shaking violently, as he stood on the mandala pattern, in the centre of the carpet. At this, the little boy became frightened, sat up and screamed.

Although his parents reassured him at the time, the little boy was told when he was older that a Mr Booth, the funeral director, who lived in the house originally, suffered from delirium tremors which made his hands shake violently, and that he was a tall thin man. He also had a little girl, who died of a childhood illness in the house, when she was about eight or nine.

The next tale is a dream – but with ghostly undertones.

A middle-aged man visited Wycoller, an ancient Pennine weaving hamlet, full of stone cottages with mullioned windows, now much tarted up, and a tourist haven. It is an isolated spot, above the River Colne in Lancashire, and at the time of the visit, still relatively undiscovered.

The man had a strange sensation of 'déja vu' when he visited the hamlet for the first time. The houses, stream, and old pack horse bridge, all seemed somehow familiar. He described the area as having a strange spiritual quality, and feeling that he belonged there, or somewhere very like it.

Soon after he had a dream. He was back in Wycoller, although a much earlier Wycoller than he remembered. Standing on a hill above the hamlet, he watched a procession come up from the moors onto the ridge. There were men in rough skins and furs, and priests in white robes. It seemed to be a very warm summer's day, and children in the procession carried bouquets of flowers. In the middle of the group were four white oxen drawing a rough sled, which seemed to be made from branches lashed together, and on it, in a kind of bier, was the body of a young woman of about thirty years of age. Her long dark hair was parted in the middle, and plaited down to her waist. She was wearing a sleeveless frock or tunic, held by a leather girdle at the waist, and reaching to her knees, in some brown fur, possibly bearskin. The oxen had garlands of flowers around their necks, and the bier was also heaped with garlands of white and yellow flowers.

As he looked, the dreamer had a sense of shock and horror, as if the woman had died suddenly, by violence. He felt she was an important person in the local community, and that she may have been the victim of a crime of passion.

On reaching the top of the ridge, the procession paused. The woman was lifted off the bier, and handed down to a man standing in a shallow natural hollow in the ground, which was strewn with fresh green leaves. He took her in his arms, and laid her in the hollow. As the dreamer watched, the children, who seemed to belong to her, came forward, and laid their bouquets of flowers in the hollow beside her.

When he woke up after the dream, the man was struck by its vivid clarity, as he was not a person who frequently remembered dreams. On a further visit to Wycoller, he met a local historian, and asked about a burial mound not far from the hamlet. He was told it had been excavated, and the remains of a young woman had been found.

Many people have premonitions of death, but not all are specific as to its manner. In the late nineteenth century, the nurse of an infant child belonging to a well-to-do mill owning family in Northern Ireland had a very disturbing dream. She dreamt that her little charge was in a strange and terrifying landscape, heavy with menace. As she watched, helplessly calling, and trying to draw him back to safety, the earth rose up with a monstrous roar, and swallowed the child without trace. The next day she tearfully told his mother of the experience, and for many years, the pair watched the young boy like hawks, to protect him from possible harm. But he grew from youth to manhood, and his mother and old nurse forgot the dream. On the outbreak of the First World War he joined an Ulster regiment, and during the Battle of the Somme, he was lost in action during heavy bombardments. A comrade said the last time he was seen, was just before an enormous explosion buried half the platoon alive. They had been advancing over no-man's-land, that hideously defiled landscape of craters, mud and splintered trees, a hell on earth, where grass never had time to grow before the next salvo churned it up again. Here, then, the premonition of an infant's nurse, a full generation before, had come to fulfilment.

Although most of the foregoing stories are hearsay, and cannot be checked, in many cases, with the people involved, they are fairly typical of paranormal experiences which could be repeated ad infinitum. I mention them merely as examples of what I have heard.

My own experiences have been less dramatic, but no less interesting. I have personally refuted (or so I hope) the legend of Cadair Idris, a haunted mountain in Mid Wales. According to the legend, anyone who spends a night on the mountain will see the day dawn blind, mad, or a poet.

The lowering peaks of Cadair Idris, said to hide the Brenin Llwyd, a flying monster.

A group of students from Aberystwyth had recently been to test the theory, and were frightened by "strange noises" among the rocks. So as a feature for my newspaper, I trekked up the mountain with Bob Staniforth, the photographer, his cameras, a tape recorder, and a tent.

Sunset on Cadair Idris

We set up our tent beneath the lowering crags of Arthur's chair, just as the sun went down over Bardsey Island in the West. There are some startlingly white sheep on Cadair Idris, but apart from them we saw no fairies (recorded), lake monsters (alleged), Brenin Llwyd (a kind of gloomy pterodactyl), or anything supernatural. We did see the most gloriously clear expanse of the Milky Way I have ever seen – there seemed to be more stars than sky, and in the course of the night, fortified with Clan Dew, Bob and I enjoyed a conversation of almost telepathic rapport.

In the morning, we dutifully made our way to the summit, and, satisfied that there were no monsters there either, we clambered down into the town of Dolgellau, passing surprised early morning walkers on the descent, to report to our newsdesk on the night's vigil. On the phone I gained the faintest suspicion that the News Editor had been hoping that we might both be deranged by the morning, but I think he probably thought we were mad to go up in the first place. But then we probably were. One camper who tried it was found wandering, suffering from temporary blindness, and his tent was discovered torn to shreds. Or so they say. Anyway, the angel must have passed us by that night, like the Israelites in Egypt. Certainly, the Brenin Llwyd, which was thought to have carried off a young Welsh boy in the 1900s (his footprints ended in the snow, and cries were heard receding above) did not put in an appearance.

I once spent a night-long vigil on a Tudor four-poster bed, in the haunted bedroom of an ancient manor house in Yorkshire, waiting for the ghost of a cavalier killed in a duel in 1684.

Oakwell Hall, at Birstall, was started in the time of the Wars of Roses, saw the encampment of a Royalist host during the Civil War, and was sacked by Roundhead soldiers in 1643, after their defeat at the battle of Adwalton Moor, about a mile distant. It was romanticised by Charlotte Brontë as 'Fieldhead' in her novel Shirley, after she had lived there for a time, when it was used as a private school.

The Oakwell ghost is reputed to be Willam Batt, a former squire, who was killed in a duel at Barnet near London, just before Christmas in 1684. The first his family knew of it was when the sound of galloping hooves approached the Hall, the main door swung open, and a dark cloaked figure with a very pale face strode across the threshold into the lattice-

Winter sunlight creates a ghostly effect on panelling and a portrait of Charles II at haunted Oakwell Hall.

windowed Great Hall, past the startled family gathered around a roaring log fire, and purposefully up the stairs, towards the major bedroom. Recognising the silent visitor as William, the family followed in trepidation, noticing a bloodstained trail on the stairs, and a bloody footprint near the bedroom door, which was closed. A search of the rest of the hall discovered no-one, and he seemed to have vanished into thin air.

News came soon after that the unfortunate squire had been killed on the very day that his relatives had seen him at the Hall. His body was brought back to Yorkshire, and he was buried at Birstall Church on December 30.

A stain by the bedroom door is said to be the ineradicable bloody footprint left by the unhappy cavalier, and many people have heard or seen something in the week before Christmas around the Hall. A previous curator, John Lidster, once stepped aside for a shadowy figure. Slowly, he became aware that there was no-one present in the corridor except himself.

Above: Oakwell Hall, West Yorkshire. Right: Steve Cliffe prepares to retire with photographer Bob Staniforth's lens bag artistically rearranged as a "nightcap".

On another occasion he was setting up a camera to photograph the haunted major bedroom when he thought someone entered the room. Assuming it was his wife, he said hello without looking up. When he did so, no-one was there.

Bob Staniforth and I went to the Hall on midwinter night, the 21st of December. Oakwell stood dark and silent, framed by skeletal trees as we approached. Our car headlights swept the many darkened windows, concealing the quiet mystery within. A torch cut through the darkness, and a tall figure beckoned us to follow. Down tangled pathways we went, entering the Hall, and along creaking corridors of dark oak.

Our guide, ex-policeman, Derek Copley, then curator of Oakwell, showed us to the haunted bedroom. "Sooner you than me," he said, glancing about. "Sometimes when I'm out walking the dog late at night, I look up at the Hall. I've never seen anything, but I've a good imagination," he smiled.

It was the first time anyone had slept in the Hall for fifty years – and no-one knows how long it had been since anyone slept on the four-poster, with its heavily-carved bedposts and draped canopy. Around the edge of the bed-frame were sockets, where candles could be set when the bed doubled as a bier for deceased occupants. I wondered how many times this had been the case in its four-hundred-year-old history. I would have shuddered, but Mr Copley had thoughtfully left the central heating on.

In a wood-panelled room quite close to the bedroom was a collection of cannon balls and weapons – mementos of the Battle of Adwalton nearby. After their defeat enraged Roundheads had broken down the front door of the Hall, and pillaged the place, looking for the Royalist owners. Whether they were present or not is unknown, but a romantic story insists that they escaped via a secret passage from what is now the haunted bedroom. I have seen this. It appears to be a medieval loo – a narrow stone shaft, concealed in a closet behind the panelling, and probably the origin of "strange" sensations of cold (draughts) experienced by visitors near the bedroom door.

On the night of our vigil, I wandered down, through the shadowy Hall, past carved oaken chests and brass candelabra, to the front door where the ghost had made its dramatic entry. Here, in 1643, the Roundheads had burst down the door, and the wooden shaft, or bolt, which secures it, is a replacement, whereas the one on the rear door is original, so enduring were the artefacts of old (Civil Wars excluded).

Turning from the door I caught my breath. An indistinct shape loomed dimly on the old staircase across the Great Hall – just where the ghost had left its trail of blood! Gathering composure, I moved forward, studying the object carefully. It was a very heavy bunch of mistletoe, hung above the stair by an optimistic would-be reveller.

Back in the bedroom, we settled down for the night, tape recorder at the ready, dozing fitfully in our sleeping bags on the four-poster. Sleep was difficult as innumerable ticking clocks chimed in an un-concerted orchestration of disharmony every quarter hour. In the small hours bumping noises were heard, and what sounded like a banging door. We know that the only person with access to the Hall was the curator, as we were, in fact, locked in.

"It's the clock mechanism," said Bob sensibly – unwilling to stir from his sleeping bag. I too didn't fancy leaving the security of the four-poster. The hour hand on the grandfather clock in the corner crept round until the first streaks of a pink dawn lit the Eastern sky. Our tape recorder lay unused.

Derek Copley came in with the dawn – making sufficient noise to let us know he was not a ghost, and the bacon sandwiches he brought with him were gratefully received. We had not seen or heard anything definite – and most old houses make strange noises at night ...

"The ghost must have come while we were asleep," suggested Bob. It must have, because we didn't go to see who was there when the door banged!

Emily Brontë wrote the famous novel *Wuthering Heights*, which despite its quaint literary style is a classic. It is the story of a fruitless love scattered to the four winds on the barren Yorkshire moors.

Heathcliff, tormented by Cathy's wraith, forever tapping for admittance through the window of his mind, is driven to despair and death. When their graves lie side by side, in the moorland turf, where they loved to romp as wayward children, the story is not ended, and their spirits are seen together on the moor.

Few people know that, in reality, the figure of a girl, resembling Emily in age and appearance is supposed to have been seen, walking the moors to the Brontë waterfall. This haunting was partly responsible for the tourist boom, which has brought visitors from all over the world to the gritty valley and town of Haworth, to see the grim parsonage where the Brontë sisters lived.

There is also a cottage, close to the parsonage, which I have visited. Here, the local vicar prevented a scheduled exorcism, after the owner claimed to have been disturbed by the apparition of a young girl. The cottage had been converted into a small restaurant, and the owner, Mr Keith Akeroyd, was surprised one day by a rustling noise. Turning, he saw the figure of a young woman, smiling and giggling at him. She then walked across the room to where a flight of stairs used to be, and disappeared. Running up the new stairs, Mr Akeroyd said he again met the spectral visitor, standing in the bedroom, "chuckling and smiling". Thereafter, the visitation reoccurred every December 19 – the date of Emily's death in 1848. A study of portraits confirmed the visitor as Emily. The vicar of Haworth who prevented the exorcism told me: "Although I wouldn't go so far as to say I don't believe in such things, I've never seen a ghost. I saw Mr Akeroyd, and I visited the place, but I didn't think that an exorcism was necessary."

A subsequent owner of the cottage, Mr Colin Rushworth, was planning to hold an all-night vigil to spot the wraith, when I spoke to him. Whether he was successful I don't know, but ghosts are always good business.

As far as is known, Emily Brontë never had a lover, and lived a rather claustrophobic life, among fairly unsophisticated people, in a cut-off, remote valley, of the bleak and rain-lashed Pennines, which must have been pretty grim – even if your father wasn't a touchy, eccentric, Victorian parson, and hers was!

Emily's joy was to roam the moors as a child, with her brother, Branwell – perhaps the more kindly moors of summer, in between the rain storms and low cloud. Emily and Branwell were very close – like Cathy and Heathcliff, who also loved the moors. When Branwell, disappointed by lack of success, took to drink in later life, it was Emily who defended him from the critical Charlotte, and supported him home, through the streets of Haworth. She was heartbroken at his graveside, when he died at only 31; catching a chill, it is said, in the churchyard, she too, followed her brother into the dank tomb in Haworth Parish Church, within a few months.

The love expressed in Wuthering Heights seems to be the love of frustrated childhood romance, the thwarted joy and expectation of unfettered youth, which howls in anguish from the pages of a remarkable book. Maybe Emily too had her secret – the story behind the story of Cathy and Heathcliff's love.

Perhaps I can end this chapter with the tale of how I was once mistaken for a ghost – or rather how a ghost was mistaken for me!

When I was a teenager, I was in the habit of visiting an old building, formerly a row of cottages, which had been converted into a small engineering workshop, and then a garage. Known as 'The Dell', it occupied a dank hollow of a river valley, on the edge of a small manufacturing town in Cheshire. Its deeds went back to 1642, the year the Civil War started, and it was built of crumbling red sandstone and brick, some of which might have been part of the fabric of an earlier building on the site. At the time, it was owned by my brother, who carried on a garage business there. During the excavation of inspection pits for vehicle maintenance, both inside and outside the building, a sunken wall of heavily eroded red sandstone blocks, having no relation to the present building, and obviously very old, was discovered.

Outside, leading down from the main road, which crossed the river by modern bridges and embankments, was the remains of the old stage-coach road, leading to the now disused ford in the river. It made a sharp descent from the much higher level of the modern road, passing close by the former cottages, and then disappearing into woodland.

When my brother first acquired the premises, he was told by the previous occupier, an old man, that there had been a stage-coach accident on this road, and that on frosty nights, the dogs, which habitually ran alongside the old coaches could be heard, baying on the wind.

Forearmed with this knowledge, he, however, failed ever to hear the phenomena. But a variety of other curious incidents occurred. Objects were frequently mislaid, or disappeared. And one night, a welder working late on his own, heard a loud crash outside which so startled him that he dropped his lit torch and ran. In the morning the gas from two bottles was exhausted, and the welder never went near the place again. On another occasion a mechanic was working late, after dark, when he thought he heard footsteps approach the main door. Without looking up, he called, "In here", thinking the visitor must be a customer. When no-one came in, he held up his inspection lamp, and insists he saw a creature, about the size of a calf, and definitely not human, pass by the open door on the outside without stopping. When he reached the door and looked out into the gloom, he says he saw the shape pass by the end of the long building, but by the time he got there it had gone – apparently along the old road into the woodland. If it was a calf, it must have walked along the main road in heavy traffic for at least a half mile, as there was no other access for animals from that direction, and no stray animal was found.

A friend of my brother once offered to spend the night at The Dell. He was a man who prided himself on his logical mind. In the morning he was discovered in the rafters, where he had climbed for safety, after hearing "inexplicable" noises, which he declined to talk about. What exactly defied his "logicality", we have never been able to establish.

Old cottages, once on a coaching route, where the author was mistaken for a ghost.

I have often been alone at night in the old building, and the sounds I heard were numerous – notably the sound of mortar falling between the enormous cavity walls, the creak of wood, and the contraction of metal equipment as the temperature dropped. Unlike all the above mentioned habitués of The Dell, I never heard the phantom footsteps.

My brother frequently heard footsteps running down the drive from the main road, towards the main door, where they would stop, and no-one would appear. This usually happened when no-one was thinking about the subject of ghosts.

One night I went down to find my brother, his friend and the mechanic, in a state of excitement. "You've been down here before?" they quizzed. I had not, but, at first, they were unwilling to accept this version. However I had an alibi, and they were able to check where I had been about an hour before.

They told me they had been having a chat, when the familiar sound of footsteps was heard. These stopped at the door, without anyone entering, and immediately after, there was a loud crash. At first, they though it was the sound of a car door being slammed, and going outside, they checked all the parked vehicles. No-one was there. Because the footsteps had been so clear, and the crash so loud, they decided that someone was playing a trick on them, and that it was probably me, as no-one else knew of the ghost. Unfortunately their theory didn't stand up, and the incident remains a mystery to this day.

My own idea is that the phenomena may be connected with something older than a stage-coach crash. The road seems to have been in use since Roman times, and, being near a ford, may once have had a building on the site of The Dell to accommodate travellers and soldiers who could not cross when the river was in spate. And perhaps the phantom calf was just that – many farm animals must have passed habitually in earlier times along the road. The residue of impressions in old places and on old objects are a vital part of the business of psychic phenomena.

On the other hand, maybe the phantom calf was a large dog, as it was the dogs which were said to have been killed in the coach crash, whose baying could be heard on starlit frosty nights, according to the old man who had The Dell before my brother. His name was Topley, and he was an apprentice on the Manchester Ship Canal when it was being built. He knew the previous occupant, an old man who had been born in the house, and died there, aged 88, and he it was who passed on the story of the coach crash to Mr Topley, who passed it on to my brother. Thus, three lives spanned the transition from stage-coaches to container lorries.

Although I did not know it when I first heard this legend, large dogs, notably Dalmatians, were trained to run alongside, or between the wheels of coaches in the eighteenth and early nineteenth centuries, and were known as carriage dogs for this reason.

They can frequently be seen doing this in old illustrations and prints of coaches in motion.

The Dalmatian or Coach Dog

10

EXPLAINING GHOSTS?

There have been various attempts to explain ghosts. One of the best is to look for a normal explanation of apparently abnormal happenings. This is a frequently neglected method. For example, while writing this book, I was living in a remote farm cottage on the edge of Snowdonia, in North Wales. Our visitors were few, and the nearest neighbours were a good two fields away. Soon after we took up residence we began to notice strange bumping noises after dark – apparently coming from the adjacent byre, which was attached to the cottage. Sometimes the noises were quite loud, and gave the impression that someone was moving about. Whenever we investigated, there was no-one to be seen, although in day-light, we had noticed one or two poachers about with dogs, we never saw them at night.

It was only after we discovered a patch of feathers, two feet, and a pair of pigeon wings in the field, that we suspected a fox was about.

The bumping continued, most nights. It would start, and cease after a few minutes, never being heard twice on the same night. One day, as I was filling the outside refuse bin I noticed that a piece of the plastic bin liner had been torn off. Looking closer I discovered that the entire edge of the bin liner, where it overlapped along the top of the bin, was full of teeth marks, and had obviously been tugged and chewed off in places. The fox had been trying to extract the liner, and its contents of rotting food, causing the bin to rock, and make that "inexplicable" bumping noise on the concrete of the yard. Because the plastic lid had been securely fixed, it had never succeeded in pulling out the contents, but returned to the fruitless task every night, while doing its "rounds". The bumping therefore continued, but our apprehension, on dark winter nights, did not.

According to Walter Whatley Carington M.Sc., apparitions (ghosts, phantoms, spectres) are "telepathically induced hallucinations." These are, "externalised by the witness, with such vividness, as often to be indistinguishable from normal physical events." Whatley Carington was an exponent of the theory of telepathy, which he strove to establish as an accepted science in his book, "Telepathy; Matter, Mind, and Meaning."

Soon after it was set up, the Society for Psychical Research did a census, in 1882, of 17000 people, and found that 1,684 or 9.9 per cent had paranormal experiences to report, which is about one in every ten people. Of those cases involving apparitions of persons known to the witness, one in 43 occurred within 12 hours of the death of the person seen, when a chance factor suggested that the proportion should have been one in 19000.

Four main categories of apparitions were discovered:

1. Apparitions of living persons, who consciously projected their image to a place where they were seen by another person, known to them.

2. Crisis apparitions of people – seen in another place, when they were in emotional extremity, or at the point of death.

3. Post-mortem apparitions of people, known to those who saw them, after their deaths.

4. Hauntings of persons, not known by those who see them, regularly in certain places, but not elsewhere.

Most apparitions are reported to behave in a dazed, drugged, somnam-bulistic fashion – as if they are, "not all there". Hauntings by the form of ghost designated as an apparition (excluding poltergeists, demons, etc) are regarded as false if some physical action is carried out, leaving behind an effect, such as an entry in a log book, or a borrowed anorak, neatly folded on top of a grave.

The process of seeing an apparition is described as similar to that involved in psychometry – the reading of the history of an object by handling it, practiced by some mediums. The theory is that the object calls up in the mind of the sensitive, ideas, and images, connected with it. In cases where figures in hauntings are seen recurrently in particular surroundings, the whole building, walls, furniture, etc, may tend to call up in the mind of anyone who perceives them, whatever ideas have been associated with them by other minds.

So it may be that the image of a particular figure, going through particular movements, such as lighting the fire, had been closely associa-ted in the mind of some former occupant of the house. When the surroundings, or objects, are watched by a new occupant, they will tend to call up images of the figure already associated with them. Someone poking a fire, or sitting in a chair, for example.

This explanation can cover cases where furniture is removed from one place to another – and the ghost moves too! As perhaps in the case of "Old Joe" and the chair from the Duke of Clarence? But the idea is inappropriate, if not inadequate, when it comes to explaining the projected images of the living.

Experiments have been conducted with persons with a certain faculty, termed "eidectic imagery", which is the ability to construct, or superimpose on external reality, an image, from the mind's eye, of such vivid clarity it is indistinguishable from physical reality, at least in the mind of the projector. However, such people have been able to succeed in projecting images of themselves to distant places, like the apartments of friends, who actually reported seeing them there, in the form of an apparition.

It is further postulated that the only type of person who is "able" to see ghosts is such a person with an eidectic image-making faculty. These are able to respond far more readily to the suggestions of images inherent in old objects and places, termed by psychic investigators "Ks", which were originated in the mind's eye of some former, habitual, observer of the scene, or person, reproduced in the form of an apparition. An objection to this, is that most things must have a multitude of possible Ks superimposed upon them, and must tend to cancel one another out. The way of getting round this argument is the postulation that in order to see the right K, there must be a natural rapport, or like-minded temperament, between the percipient, and the originator of the K.

However, the next objection I can think of to this theory is how do people who see the projected image of a living person manage it without being eidectic image makers? The answer is "something to do with telepathy." One further point about eidectic imagery. Are people born with this gift, or is it a faculty which can be developed, can come or go in the course of life? I believe there are those who are naturally inclined in this direction, but that others can also develop a less perfect version.

In the case of K-based apparitions, the theory is that what is seen is not the deceased person, or persons, surviving in totality – but merely a fragment, worked up by the mind of the percipient – "a feebly autonomous psychic effigy". This is thought to be so because even though the apparition may have simple vestiges of speech, and movement, it does not have full autonomy – in the sense that it *cannot respond* to the witness, either visually or verbally.

This, however, is not the case with apparitions of the living, or crisis apparitions, of which there are many examples, and which frequently convey some intelligible message, verbal or otherwise, to the witness. The "explanation" of this series comes under the general heading of telepathy, which I will examine in a moment.

G.N.M. Tyrrell, in his work, "Apparitions", stated: "There is usually a way of evading a survivalist explanation, but I think if we are candid, we must admit, that as the cases mount up, these explanations have the air of being rather a ragged set of makeshifts, and that a good many cases, regarded apart from á priori considerations, do point to a surviving agency." Tyrrell believed that in some cases of apparitions, notably in the frequent cases reported of persons recently deceased, the "initiating telepathic agency" for the phenomena, was the dead person, and not the mind of the percipient, or psychometry.

The psychologist, C.G. Jung suggested the possibility of the human psyche being, in a degree, independent of bodily functions, and based this on a number of medical cases, where a patient had suffered acute cerebral collapse, and was, to all appearances, in deep coma, yet at the same time retained complicated psychic processes – normally attributed to brain activity, when no such activity could, medically speaking, have taken place. He cites examples where people were also able to "see" what was going on around them, frequently from "out of the body" angles, and viewpoints. And in one case, the patient had subsequently verifiable ESP.

In his book, "Synchronicity", Jung gives these examples.

One of Jung's patients had undergone a very difficult childbirth. When the doctor attending her had gone, and the nurse was about to leave, the patient said she suddenly felt as if she was sinking through the bed into a bottomless void. She tried to speak but couldn't. The nurse hurried to the bedside, and began feeling for her pulse, which she seemed to have difficulty finding, by the way she moved her fingers to and fro. Jung described the scene:

"Yet she herself felt quite alright, and was slightly amused at the nurse's alarm. She was not in the least frightened. The next thing she was aware of was that, without feeling her body and its position, she was looking down from a point in the ceiling and could see everything going on in the room below her; she saw herself lying in the bed, deadly pale, with closed eyes. Beside her stood the nurse. The doctor paced up and down the room excitedly, and it seemed to her that he had lost his head, and didn't know what to do. Her relatives crowded to the door. Her mother and her husband came in and looked at her with frightened faces. She told herself it was too stupid of them to think she was going to die, for she would certainly come round again."

"All this time she knew that behind her was a glorious, park-like landscape shining in the brightest colours, and in particular an emerald green meadow with short grass, which sloped gently upwards beyond a wrought iron gate leading into the park. It was Spring, and little gay flowers such as she had never seen before were scattered about in the grass. The whole demesne sparkled in the sunlight, and the colours were of an indescribable splendour. The sloping meadow was flanked on both sides by dark green trees. It gave her the impression of a clearing in the forest, never yet trodden by the foot of man.

'I knew that this was the entrance to another world, and that if I turned round to gaze at the picture directly, I should feel tempted to go in at the gate, and thus step out of life.' "

"She did not actually see this landscape, but knew it was there. She felt that there was nothing to stop her from entering in through the gate. She only knew that she would turn back to her body, and would not die. That was why she found the agitation of the doctor, and the distress of her relatives stupid and out of place. The next thing that happened was that she awoke from her coma and saw the nurse bending over her in bed. She was told that she had been unconscious for about half an hour. The next day, some fifteen hours later, when she felt a little stronger, she made a remark to the nurse about the incompetent and 'hysterical' behaviour of the doctor during her coma. The nurse energetically denied this criticism in the belief that the patient had been completely unconscious at the time and therefore could have known nothing of the scene. Only when she described in full detail what had happened during the coma, was the nurse obliged to admit that the patient had perceived the events as they happened in reality."

Jung added: "One would expect such obvious cerebral anaemia to militate against, or prevent the occurrence of highly complex psychic processes of that kind."

"Sir Auckland Geddes presented a very similar case before the Royal Medical Society on February 26, 1927, though here the ESP went very much further. During a state of collapse, the patient noted a splitting off of an integral consciousness from his bodily consciousness, the latter gradually resolving itself into its organ components. The other consciousness possessed verifiable ESP."

Jung also quoted the cases of soldiers suffering acute brain injuries: "Contrary to all expectations, a severe head injury is not always followed by a corresponding loss of consciousness. To the observer, the wounded man seems apathetic, "in a trance", and not conscious of anything. Subjectively, however, consciousness is by no means extinguished.

"Sensory communication with the outside world is in a large measure restricted, but is not always completely cut off, although the noise of battle, for instance, may suddenly give way to a, "solemn silence". In this state there is sometimes a very distinct and impressive feeling, or hallucination, of levitation, the wounded man seeming to rise into the air in the same position he was in at the moment he was wounded. If he was wounded standing up, he rises in a standing position, if lying down, he rises in a lying position, if sitting, he rises in a sitting position. Occasionally his surroundings seem to rise with him – for instance the whole bunker in which he finds himself at the moment.

"The height of the levitation may be anything from eighteen inches to several yards. All feeling of weight is lost. In a few cases the wounded think they are making swimming movements with their arms. If there is any perception of their surroundings at all, it seems to be mostly imaginary, i.e. composed of memory images. During levitation the mood is predominantly euphoric. 'Buoyant, solemn, heavenly, serene, relaxed, blissful, expectant, exciting,' are the words used to describe it ... "

Jung put forward two suggestions to explain these phenomena.

The first was that while the brain is paralysed, and normal mental activities cease, during coma, the sympathetic system, ruling the operation of heart, lungs, etc, keeps going, and may be capable of a form of consciousness, including thoughts and perceptions of its own. He cites the case of experiments done with bees, by Karl Von Frisch, who showed that although bees have no cerebrospinal system, they can communicate information about the direction and distance of a food source, by a sort of dance, to other bees. This seems to be a conscious and intentional act, of which insects, with only a sympathetic nervous system, are supposed to be incapable. Therefore how much more might the sympathetic system of a human being be conscious of? Jung argued that dreams, therefore, were not so much a product of sleeping brain cortex, as of the unsleeping sympathetic system. The psyche was the soul of the body, not the brain!

His second suggestion, was that the psychic processes of the mind were not, "mere secretions of the brain", but existed alongside, and not as a result of, the organic processes of the body, in what he termed an "acausal, synchronistic relationship."

This second idea might shed light on some of the phenomena with which we have been dealing in this book, as it suggests the possibility of psychic manifestations, not dependant on the body, which normally support them. This is to say "out of body" experiences.

Jung defined synchronistic events as relatively independent of space and time, covering such phenomena as ESP, and precognition. His own view was that ESP had been scientifically proven by the experiments of J.B. Rhine and others. It seemed, that given sufficient emotional incentive, human beings were capable of "producing" paranormal manifestations, such as correctly guessing the identity of playing cards, receiving telepathic messages, intuiting disasters, or the winners of horse races.

Most religious systems have a belief in the existence of a human "soul" – an indestructible, immortal, "divine spark", which can survive after the death of the physical body. In many traditions these are also regarded as the source of apparitions, or ghosts – being the shades of the dead. It is a fairly modern idea to attribute ghostly visitations to some kind of image recording, of little more substance than the picture on a television screen. And, in fact, according to G.N.M. Tyrrell, the authority on psychic phenomena, an apparition may be triggered by some surviving vestige of a deceased person, which has the power to act on the human mind.

A variety of other more recent theories centre around the mysterious field of electromagnetism. Some investigators claim that in most hauntings, a "cold spot" can be located, and that this is the seat of an electromagnetic phenomenon, controlling the ghostly manifestations. However I have rarely experienced this in my investigations, and I have never read anything offering conclusive evidence on the subject. But I am inclined to think that if energies are at work in some phenomena – notably poltergeist manifestations, they are probably not familiar electromagnetic waves, but something finer, less tangible, possibly of a much higher order, and registering weakly on instruments, if at all.

A member of the Society for Psychical Research, Tony Cornell, has run details of 500 cases through computer analysis, and the common denominator of poltergeist activity he discovered was a state of emotional tension among the relationships of the people involved. He also, incidentally, has never seen an apparition, despite having investigated 250 cases personally. But he has witnessed poltergeist activity. On one occasion he watched a large front door key disappear from the lock – only to discover it in the enamel mug from which he was drinking tea!

Tony Cornell's interest in the paranormal began when he was on shore leave from the Royal Navy in India. He had heard of a fakir who lived on a nearby mountain, and decided to see the man for himself. He discovered the holy man near the summit, seated beside a raging torrent 25 feet wide. After answering questions, the fakir told Cornell to look at some distant hills. When he turned back again, he was stunned to see the holy man standing on the other side of the raging torrent, without even the hem of his garment being wet. Later, when he understood more about the paranormal, Cornell wondered if it had been a trick of hypnosis, but he has since discovered that he is one of those people who cannot be hypnotised. So he still doesn't know what happened on that mountain outside Bangalore, but it kindled interest.

There is a vast body of Eastern literature devoted to the concept of developing, in life, some enduring, intangible vehicle of consciousness – which will survive death. Jung did a lot of work interpreting this according to Western psychology. Buddhists, Hindus and Taoists all subscribe to these ideas, whereas the somewhat simpler Christian view – from the fourth century onwards, was that man was born with an immortal soul, which did not perish at physical death. It is interesting to consider, however, that previous to that time, Christians believed that only God could give any form of existence to the dead again – at the Day of Judgement. Yet there has been no culture, or people, who did not believe in ghosts, or fear the spirits of the dead.

In a famous Taoist tract, "The Secret of the Golden Flower", the means by which an immortal body can be created is discussed:

"If thou wouldst complete the diamond body with no outflowing,
Diligently heat the roots of consciousness and life.
Kindle the light in the blessed country ever close at hand,
And there hidden, let thy true self always dwell."

The "blessed country" is an inward country, of the "inner way", and an object of concentration in Eastern meditation techniques.

Jung interpreted this as an "inversion of libido", which speeded up processes in the unconscious mind of the individual, bringing about

Psychologist C.G. Jung believed in an immortal 'part' of the psyche.

changes in the personality, of a deep and soulful kind. Whether or not it caused immortality he did not say. He, however, believed that there is an immortal "bit" in all of us, but that it was not recognisably the same as the external, whole personality. Also, it was "immortal" only in the sense of being an inherited record of ancestral memories and instincts.

Experiments carried out in Sweden with dying people resulted in their descriptions of being pulled, or drawn, at high speed, towards something, just before death. This sensation of "going through a tunnel" has also occurred with people, who, having clinically died, have been revived again to tell the tale. At the end of the tunnel is usually a bright light.

On one occasion a dying person and his bed were weighed carefully, and after death, an unaccountable weight loss was noted, of several pounds. In terms of potential and kinetic energy, this is quite a loss – described in one wildly unguarded estimate as equivalent to the power of an atomic bomb, supposing that the missing atoms had gone off in a chain reaction.

I believe that the psychic energies produced by, or acting alongside organic bodily processes, are extremely subtle, scientifically undefined, and quite possibly capable of many "paranormal" manifestations. Persons who concentrate on inner psychic processes do so at the risk of unbalancing a very delicate machine, which is quite capable of perpetrating disasters without prompting, but a few can achieve results. Gurdjieff described the human body as a factory. 'The work of the factory consists in transforming one kind of matter into another, namely the coarser matters, in the cosmic sense, into finer ones ... " The Russian mystic, who claimed to have studied over 400 religions, said that the inner teaching of them all was essentially the same.

He went on: "Inner growth, the growth of the inner bodies of man, the astral, the mental, and so on, is a material process completely analogous to the growth of the physical body ... Moreover the "astral body" requires for its growth the same substances as those necessary to maintain the physical body ... All the substances necessary for the maintenance of the life of the organism, for psychic work, for the higher functions of consciousness and the growth of the higher bodies, are produced by the organism from the food which enters it from outside.

The human organism receives three kinds of food: 1. The ordinary food we eat. 2. The air we breathe. 3. Our impressions."

The last named – impressions, or conscious awareness, is a most important feature of Gurdjieff's philosophy. Like Jung, he seems to regard awareness as the highest manifestation of life, but unlike Jung, he insists that it has to be used, in order to achieve the specific aim of building "higher bodies". This results in the creation of higher and finer gradations of energy, or substance, from which the subtle bodies are constructed. In Gurdjieff's system, energy and substance seem interchangeable. Most of his ideas are covered in P.D. Ouspensky's book, *In Search of the Miraculous*, and many are cosmological in the extreme.

G.I. Gurdjieff

Quite late in Gurdjieff's life a former disciple of his, John Bennett, renewed acquaintance with the master in Paris, and had this tale to relate. Gurdjieff had gone on a motor jaunt heading for Cannes in the summer of 1948, when in passing through a small village his car was rammed by a delivery waggon with a drunken driver, who with his passenger was instantly killed. Gurdjieff's passengers escaped injury, but he himself was pinned in the buckled car, between the wheel and the seat, from which it took an hour to extricate him. He was conscious the whole time, and directed each movement to prevent fatal loss of blood.

Bennett reached the Rue Des Colonels Renard the following evening, just as two cars drove slowly up. From one of them Gurdjieff painfully emerged, spattered with blood and black with bruises. Bennett realised that he, "was looking at a dying man. Even this is not enough to express it. It was a dead man, a corpse, that came out of the car; and yet it walked. I was shivering like someone who sees a ghost."

Later in his apartment, while he talked, a gush of blood ran from Gurdjieff's ear. Bennett thought, "he has a cerebral haemorrhage, he will kill himself if he continues to force his body to move!" But then he reflected, "he has to do all this. If he allows his body to stop moving, he will die. He has power over his body."

The doctor, on arrival, ordered Gurdjieff immediately to bed. As an old man, the mystic was in danger of dying of pneumonia, if nothing else. But the patient disobeyed and came to dinner as usual – fractured skull, smashed ribs, blood-filled lungs and all – to the extreme apprehension of those present. When he did go to bed, he refused the pain-killing morphia which had been prescribed, but by some incredible deployment of inner energy he knitted together so well again, that within two weeks, he was back to his habitual routines.

Even when Gurdjieff died the following year, he did so attended by curious manifestations. Solito Solano, another of his disciples wrote: "Four hours after his death, his forehead and neck were still very warm; the doctor said he couldn't understand it."

After the embalming Bennett, who had come on the first plane from England said: "Although no-one else was in the chapel, I was convinced that he was breathing. When I shut my eyes, and held my breath, I could distinctly hear a regular breathing."

Gurdjieff's organs were so badly deteriorated, doctors were amazed that he could have kept alive as long as he did. An odd incident also accompanied the funeral service in the Greek Orthodox Church. Madame de Hartmann wrote: "When the priest finished the ceremony, and entered the altar, the electric lights suddenly and inexplicably went out, plunging the church into darkness, illuminated only by little candles burning before images." The rest of the funeral service passed off normally, except for the force of overwhelming grief, so great, that even the undertaker wept at the graveside.

Gurdjieff was more familiarly known by his followers for an ability to transfer energy directly to people who needed it, as in the case of the sick, the tired, or those making a special effort in some task. Bennett once described how this happened to him, and how he felt himself "capable of anything," under its influence. Gurdjieff's powers were never adequately explained solely by his undoubted ability as a hypnotist. He seemed to be a genuine manifestor and practitioner of energy transference. Some believed him to be well over a hundred years old.

It is my view that this type of energy may be an "enabling" substance, which powers the phenomena of ghosts, demons and nature spirits, as experienced by human beings.

On one hand, it has been argued that apparitions, at least, are telepathically induced hallucinations, brought through a kind of selective image-recording system in the fabric of old objects, such as buildings, furniture, etc. But this in itself is not sufficient explanation for all the accompanying manifestations of genuine cases of apparitions. I agree with Lethbridge in his idea that the distinct tingling, and hair bristling sensations, coupled with a feeling of intense cold, in the victim of such an experience, signify that an energy drain of some kind is taking place – and that this, in fact, is what powers the manifestation.

In three examples given at length in this book – the Duke of Buckingham ghost, the modern-day demon, and the Allor Moloch cromlech, these sensations were noted. I might add that until I experienced the possibility myself, I never took it seriously. If an energy drain takes place, one must postulate the existence of a negative vortex, or something like it, into which energy may drain, bringing alive an inherent image, vestige or archetypal manifestation. Thus, if positive energy flows into negative vortex with any frequency, one may expect an increasingly powerful and frequent manifestation of the influence, and an increasingly debilitating, and dangerous effect of the energy loss. The victim will be drained of energy, while the tormenting manifestation gains in power. Unless something is done to effectively break the circuit, the result may even be tragic. In the case of the demon a magic ritual was performed and broke the spell – accompanied by the destruction of the object, around which the negative force clung. In the case of the Duke of Buckingham ghost, the negative circuit may not have been broken. Religious and magical practices give examples of healing as well as destructive forces. The science of subtle energies seems to be that they can be made to "flow" in either direction. Like electricity, they can be beneficial or destructive in application, and they obey laws of their own, of which most, if not all of us, are quite ignorant.

The vast majority of psychic phenomena can be put down to mistakes in judgement, suggestibility, imagination, hysteria and so on. But a hard core of phenomena stand apart. Who are the people who see ghosts? Are they special people, or like you and me?

An authority on telepathy said that the connecting link could be a universal consciousness of ideas – through the human "sub conscious". Jung postulated the existence of a "Collective Unconscious" to which all minds were linked.

Some people have a naturally better access to this than others. It has been suggested that telepathy may be a primitive vestige of a faculty still actively operating among less civilised cultures today – like the Australian Aborigines, who are thought to be able to communicate emotional tones to one another over great distance. Usually the signals are simple, indicating danger, for instance, and not complex ideas. Hives of bees exhibit the same common consciousness. In the modern world, slogans, symbols and emblems still have their effect on the group or community mind, through the ideas associated with them.

Perhaps some people are more receptive to certain frequencies of signals than others, dependent on the right conditions, and perhaps they are also more at risk ...

Not everyone would wish to agree with an expert on telepathic research who said:

"It may be that the virtual merger of individual personalities, such as telepathic processes are likely to promote, or facilitate, especially in the absence of physical bodies, may be the central feature of the psychological destiny of man."

In theory almost anyone could be capable of seeing a ghost – in practice, only certain people do. Is this just because they "happened to be there", as in the case of Harry Martindale, and the Roman ghosts? Harry, who claimed he was not psychic, and didn't wish to know of such things?

Or is there a more stable pattern underlying it all?

The Spiritualists would certainly have us believe so, with their realms of the dead, elemental spirits and so on. Conan Doyle, the creator of Sherlock Holmes, was a great promoter of the so-called Knottingley Fairies – since proven to be a photographic fraud by the confession of one of the two little girls involved. Admittedly, Conan Doyle could have been an innocent victim of the hoax, but to be fooled by children does not say much for his scientific spirit of inquiry.

However there are many interesting features of Spiritualism, not least the "voices", which come through a good medium, which are not entirely satisfactorily explained by "hysteria", fragmentation of personality, and so on.

For instance, it has been fashionable for people in the congregations of certain Christian churches to stand up and "speak in tongues". To the casual listener this may sound like prime gibberish, and those others in the congregation, who offer themselves as interpreters, may be presumptuous to say the least.

But consider this story, which was related to me. A Chinese student was invited to attend the congregation of a Pentecostal church in this country. In the course of a meeting, a member of the congregation stood up and began a discourse "in tongues", whereupon the Chinese student walked out. When asked afterwards what was wrong, he was quite indignant, saying that the speaker had used the worst language he had ever heard, having uttered a foul string of abuse – in Mandarin Chinese!

For those not familiar with the process, may I explain that most "speakers in tongues" are unaware of the nature of their message – the idea being that the Holy Spirit is manifesting through them, as mere instruments of the Lord. If one accepts the truth of the above story, and the complete bewilderment of the people involved, one is tempted to look at Spiritualist explanations of phenomena in a new light.

Incidentally, the Apostle Paul said there was no point in speaking in tongues, unless it was in a language understood by the listener. The original meaning derived from the tongues of flame of the Holy Spirit, which came among the Disciples at Pentecost, 40 days after Christ's Ascension, enabling them to speak in the language of foreigners who were present. This is not intentionally the case in Pentecostal, and other, congregations today. Quite simply, a kind of non-speak is uttered, followed by a liberal interpretation from another member who believes he, or she, has "got the message". As a sub-conscious process, it is probably as valid as any other.

I can add further to the Spiritualist case without going overboard in their favour. My own experience with mediums has not been impressive. I once went with one, an elderly woman, to a "haunted house", and although trying to be open-minded, I observed her act in an entirely suggestible way, ask us if we had relatives with the not uncommon names of Fred, Jack, Tom and so on, finally rounding off with some pretty trite messages from the Ouija board, which were misspelt, and betraying no intimate knowledge of anyone present, other than that elicited by her direct questioning.

However the "spirit" healing sessions of the late Harry Edwards were relatively impressive. He was at pains to establish that healing could, and did take place with patients, including babies, who had no knowledge that a healing had been instituted, and therefore, faith in its results, by the subject, could not be the explanation. On occasion, such healings were instituted by post, when relatives wrote to him on behalf of the sufferer. But he also performed many direct healings. Most were of a transient nature, bringing temporary relief, but he would encourage the process in his patients, by giving them tips on self-healing through spirit energy. His views on the accumulation and direction of this, were similar to those of Gurdjieff, and other mystics, who seem to have believed that the human body could act as an accumulator for higher forces, when so directed. Having seen the results in his patients, including those who received indirect help, I believe in the process, and the good it could bring.

I will end this chapter with the story of a Christmas ghost.

A little girl was spending Christmas at her auntie's house. The house was large, commodious, and partially comprised a shop, which acted as the local general store. Normally life was very hectic and exciting at the store, especially at Christmas, with many people coming and going, and the smell of baking, and confectionery being prepared. This year, although many relatives were present, and people hurried in and out of the shop, it was as if a damper had been put on the spirit of the occasion. The relatives communicated in whispers, and visitors spoke in an undertone. Somehow the very light of Christmas was shut out by drawn blinds.

Although she knew "something was not right", the little girl, who was very young, had no idea what was wrong. She was mystified by the nervous behaviour of her aunt, who, on hearing the cat knock something over upstairs, jumped up, crying, "Oh, my dad. My dad!"

She, "seemed to be the only little girl in the house," according to her recollection, and was put to bed downstairs, although normally on visits, she slept upstairs in a spare room. On Christmas Eve she had a strange dream. At least it must have been a dream, but it didn't seem like one. It seemed too real.

She was standing on the landing at the top of the stairs. How she got there, she didn't know, or understand, as she knew she had been put to bed downstairs. But there, in front of her, was Father Christmas, large as life, red robes, and white whiskers. He was holding her by the shoulders, and gently shaking her, in a friendly way, while his merry blue eyes stared into hers, twinkling in the light. They were very, very, blue, and bright – just like her Grandfather's. And as Father Christmas continued to smile, and his eyes continued to twinkle. The little girl realised something was very wrong about this situation. She felt an overwhelming fear, and apprehension, and she wanted to be away from this merry stare, and friendly grasp, back in her bed. Downstairs.

The next thing she knew, she was awake, and her parents were telling her that, "it must have been your Auntie Polly dressed up." But she knew it wasn't. The next day they brought her Grandfather downstairs from the spare room, for the funeral. And later, when she was older, she understood that he was already dead, when she saw him, dressed as Father Christmas on the upstairs landing, with his very blue eyes twinkling so merrily.

My mother had always felt that what happened was not "just a dream", and I believe her.

11

CRADLE TO GRAVE

Not far from where I used to live, in Manchester, stands the smoke-blackened edifice of a Unitarian church. Every day, thousands of people hurry by, rushing to or from work; on one of the busiest commuter routes of the city; few sparing a glance for the sooty spire, so eloquent of Victorian aspiration to the hereafter, or noticing the splendid, ornate tomb, jutting up in proud isolation, in the otherwise empty churchyard.

On it is no legend explaining the mystery, or telling to whom the impressive granite steps, or graceful white marble arches and Gothic roof, empillaring a large granite sarcophagus, are dedicated. All around is desolation. The sooty tombs of lesser notables having been removed when the churchyard was "beautified" in the sixties. Now only the rank grasses, elder, and hawthorn, speak of the churchyard's ecclesiastical decay. But nearby, light is cast on the dim history of this once-thriving community, its church, and the tomb of its founder. A bronze plaque, not yet prised off the wall by itinerant vandals, depicts the silent slumberer in the tomb, as he appeared in the full flood of life, hair swept heroically back, Victorian whiskers bristling, he poses, head and shoulders, as if for a sepia-tinted photograph of the time. On one hand an angel stretches out an arm, to crown him with a laurel wreath, on the other stands the figure of Vulcan, hammer resting idly on his anvil, his free hand covering his eyes in grief. Beneath the famous motto, "erected in grateful and appreciative remembrance, by members of his work-force", is a potted history. The man's name was Peacock, appropriately enough. He was born in the 1820s and died in the 1880s, having been master of a thriving foundry nearby, (hence Vulcan, the smith), and an MP for the East Manchester division. He was, "ever a friend of the poor," active in, "raising them to higher things".

Having done so, though, and spent his life during one of the most self-confident periods ever to create a glow of satisfaction in British history, he was unwilling to commit his body to the soil. The terms of his will ensured that he would lie above ground, in the giant granite sarcophagus, with his baroque tomb a constant reminder, to those who knew, of vanished greatness. And a puzzle to those who did not.

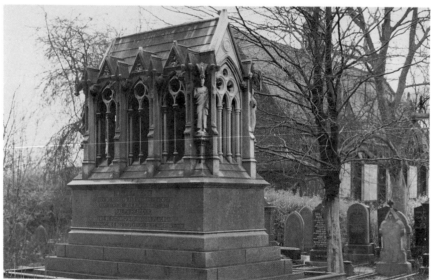

The Peacock family grave in Gorton; a true Gothic horror.

This strange reluctance , of those so hot in religion during life, to embrace the hereafter without some shred of material comfort to sustain their passage is not confined to the materialistic, grasping, and splendidly innovative Victorians. It is a fear Man has exhibited with plentiful examples from the earliest cultures.

As a young reporter my eye was caught by a small red brick enclosure in a field on my "patch". After inquiring, I discovered it was the final resting place of a non-conformist minister, the Rev. Robert Robinson, who died in 1791. He had been buried there, only a few hundred yards from his own house, in order that his daughter could come and check, every day, by means of a glass panel on the coffin lid, which remained accessible, to see if her father had "revived", and required assistance. This was made a condition of his will, and .of the inheritance he bequeathed to her. She was stated to have carried it out diligently. The Rev. Robinson never revived, and the tomb was eventually filled in. But the wall surrounding it, in the field at Romiley in Cheshire, still remained, as a grim reminder of an eccentric clergyman's final wish. It has since been demolished and his remains were exhumed in February 1991.

When workmen broke into the tomb and most of the icy water had been pumped out, I was invited to go and have a look inside. As I walked down the sloping trench to the base of the monument, I felt as if I were entering Hell. "He won't want to go in there!" someone yelled. "Course he will, he's an historian", replied my host, the cemeteries superintendent.

I leant through the broken aperture, smearing my elbows with the limey white mortar builders used 200 years ago. A strange gaseous smell of damp and decay hung in the air and a sudden sadness oppressed my spirits, as heavy and leaden as the coffin liners, which, distorted and filled with water, held the final, mortal, remains of Dr. Robinson, his wife and daughter. I was thankful that the enveloping waters, dark and opaque, hid from view the jumble of bones.

Originally the tomb must have been a mausoleum, built to stand above ground. It had spy holes on either side, to allow Dr. Robinson's relatives to check daily on the state of his coffin. For those were the days of grave-robbers who sold corpses for anatomical experiments. As an added precaution, his coffin was bricked inside a stone box tomb inside the vault. There was also the remains of a doorway into the tomb, blocked with stone. The level of the ground had been raised at some time, possibly to deter vandals, and water drainage levels had risen with it, flooding the vault.

Top: Workmen tunnelled into Dr Robinson's grave; Bottom: Interior of vaulted tomb, showing spy-hole at top right. (Mark Matthews). Opposite: the lead coffin liners and the bones of the Robinson family being prepared for re-burial.

Workmen removed the remains of three skeletons (see left) for reburial in a single coffin elsewhere. A crudely-cut leaden cross found in the tomb was reburied with them. The site is scheduled for a housing development. Clearly the family's fears of desecration were not groundless after all.

There are numerous examples from history of a similar theme – at some necropolis-scale tomb "settlements" out in the desert, the dead not only had their utensils, clothes, and food, but also treasure, their very servants in some cases, and a hieroglyphic description of their descent into the underworld buried with them!

In more primitive cultures than the Egyptians, the bones of the dead were sometimes deliberately broken to prevent them "walking" after death. Sometimes the head is found at the feet of the skeleton, (*detaching the head is connected with the idea of it as the seat of the soul*) and there was a tendency to break weapons, pots, and utensils, buried with the corpse, or even to burn it, and them, to ashes.

The idea of having to placate, or ward off the displeasure of the dead, is present in most cultures. Although William the Conqueror's naked corpse was left discarded in his ransacked palace, while his erstwhile loyal followers rushed off with what ever they had grabbed, back to their own wolf-lairs, the rule of respecting the dead had been generally true, and attended by much superstition. William was finally rescued and given decent burial by monks, who appreciated the value of eminent bones.

The Vikings went to great lengths to placate their dead chiefs. Either his favourite wife, or a young girl, would be ceremonially killed and buried, or burned, with the chief. Sometimes male servants met the same fate, and one luckless retainer was killed, only to be dug up and removed, after passers-by thought they heard the old chief chanting within his mound that he didn't like the company. Afterwards, he was silent again, which must have been slight consolation to the servant! There are several Viking burial mounds on the Isle of Man. In one was discovered the skull of a young woman, with the back of her head neatly sliced off by the single blow of an axe or sword. Appropriately enough, all that remained of the old reprobate for whom this was done, were his teeth.

The Church Christianised the ancient Celtic festival of Samhain into All Hallows, or All Souls Day, on the eve of which – Hallowe'en – the souls of the dead are superstitiously believed to roam abroad, passing to the East of houses, gazing sadly at their former habitations, and the glow of warmth within. Some country people still leave offerings of food on the doorstep, so that the ghosts of former occupants may be nourished and placated by being remembered.

The dead have been thought to inhabit various places from the islands of the West, or the place of the setting sun, to the Viking underworld of Hel, the Greek Hades, or the Limbo of Roman Catholic belief. J.B. Priestley said that what was needed today, was a much clearer view of Heaven, as a place we would all confidently aspire to, as Hell was here on earth, and in its creation we might confidently tell the Devil "leave it to us!"

The Hell of the First World War, the Nazi extermination camps, and the bloody massacres in many countries of the world today, yesterday, and tomorrow, give the truth of his words. One does not have to search far to find Hell on earth, and possibly human creative genius, in the realms of science, has yet to create the biggest Dante's Inferno of them all.

But is there not, after all, some kindling of human spirit, some yearning for the transforming fire, expressed in the lure of Wagner's *Gotterdamerung* – the fiery twilight of the Gods? Norse mythology was terribly pessimistic, and so was that of the ancient Greeks. Perhaps there is a morbid satisfaction in final oblivion, beyond limbo?

In medical schools are a variety of bones, some made into complete human skeletons, to familiarise students with the human frame. Originally these were provided, after anatomical dissection, by the bodies of executed criminals, and in many cases, particularly in the late eighteenth, and early nineteenth centuries, by the bodies of the recently buried, stolen by body snatchers, and sold to medical schools. In the famous case of Burke and Hare, involving the Edinburgh Medical School, the grisly duo not only stole corpses from graveyards, but murdered to get suitable saleable specimens. So extreme was body snatching at one time that vigilante patrols guarded churchyards for miles around the vicinity of university medical schools. Burke, however, was caught, and executed for his crimes, which had caused a sensation. His body, ironically enough, was given to the medical school, and his complete skeleton can still be seen there today.

Most of the complete skeletons in such schools are not composed of the bones of any one person, but are a composite of bones from many different corpses. Whether this is in deference to the original owner, to ameliorate the squeamishness of the living in handling an entire person of unknown history, or in the hope that the baleful influences attached to the bones (get a doctor to admit to that!) cancel one another out, is difficult to say.

Bodies and their disposal have a place in Celtic and Germanic folklore. Take the mysterious case of Lindow Man, whose remains were discovered by a mechanical digger in a peat moss near Wilmslow, Cheshire in August 1984. His was not the first find in the moss – a head had been uncovered in the previous summer – leading a local man to confess to the murder of his wife. But the head was of an Iron Age Celt!

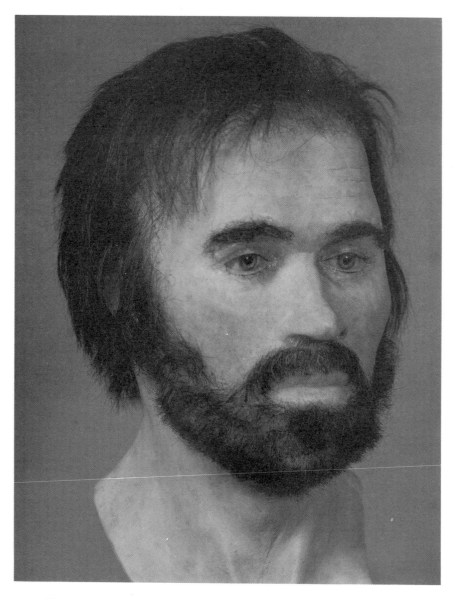

Above, a reconstruction of the features of Lindow Man (Photo: British Museum). Right: Lindow Moss as it appears today

Lindow Man's body was the best preserved, his hair and beard reddened by the peat acids which also decalcified the bones so that the
weight of peat had forced the body out of shape, particularly the head.
Sliced in half by the peat cutter, his legs and buttocks were not
recovered until four years later. Meanwhile the remains of a further
body had been discovered in February 1987 of a youth, whose missing
head was believed to be that which prompted a murder inquiry.

The "murders" however, were both nearly 2,000 years old – and are
believed by archaeologists to provide evidence of ritual human sacrifice.
Both men were apparently warriors of high social caste and had the
traces of a bright blue clay-based copper paint in their skin. These, then,
were the blue-painted naked Celtic warriors who struck terror into
Roman soldiers, as recorded by Caesar. Forensic analysis and reconstruction produced the following picture.

Lindow Man was well-built, about 25 and 5ft 6in tall, suffered from
slight arthritis and worms, had a large head with small ears and a full
head of dark hair with a beard. His finger-nails were neatly rounded,
showing he did no manual work. He had eaten wholemeal bread and
drunk water with sphagnum moss traces in it. He was naked apart from
a fox fur arm-band on his left arm, possibly a mark of status or clan.

While standing or kneeling he was struck from behind, twice, on top of the head with a narrow bladed axe. He received a vicious blow in the back which broke one of his ribs. Then a cord was tied around his neck, a stick was inserted into the cord at the back of his neck and used to twist it tighter and tighter. Unconscious but not killed by the blows on the head (the edges of the wounds were swollen), Lindow Man was now strangled and his neck was broken by the garrotte. That was the moment of death – but the executioners now slit his throat with a short deep cut at the side of the neck. That would have severed the jugular vein accentuating the showering libation of blood from the man's head. At the end of this gruesome sequence the body was dropped face downwards into a pool in the bog.

Ultimately, 2.5 metres of peat covered the body, but drainage and the removal of peat by peat cutting meant that only 1 metre remained by the time the body was recovered.

Far less is know about Lindow Youth, the second body, as it was recovered in over 70 different pieces! Unlike the older man, however, the youth had simply been beheaded. Estimates, using carbon dating, put Lindow Man's death in the 1st century AD and the youth in the 2nd century AD, that is, during the first part of the Roman occupation of Britain, indicating that Druidic practices still survived, despite the suppression of human sacrifice and destruction of the holy oak groves wherever they could be found, as happened in Anglesey.

Lindow Moss to this day is an impenetrable mass of birch thicket, growing in what would have been a treacherous peat swamp, before the system of drainage channels were dug. It is known to have had a prehistoric trackway which perhaps only the Druids knew of. It would have been ideal for their secret rites.

Sacrifices involving bog bodies are known to have occurred throughout Northern Europe from Sweden to Ireland involving Celtic and Germanic peoples. There are two aspects of Celtic veneration involved. Water-worship of springs, wells, pools and rivers is well known, many offerings of weapons and other goods have been discovered. The second element seems to concern the cult of the head which ancient Celts believed to represent divinity and the seat of the soul. Carved stone heads adorned holy places and the heads of enemies were kept.

Some writers believe the etymology of the folk demons known as boggarts or bogies with variations such as the Manx *buggane*, are an echo of the oral tradition of bog sacrifice. In Lancashire it is believed that in certain places are "hollow watchers" associated with damp watery spots and having the character of something foreboding. Was Lindow Man a sacrifice for, "the good of the community", as is suggested, or did the mistletoe pollen found in his stomach give the clue to the immortal task which had been assigned him on the "other side". Mistletoe to the Druids was the most sacred plant, representing the life force. Perhaps his watching brief may in part account for the uncanny atmosphere of the Moss to this day.

The tradition of carved stone heads survives particularly strongly in NW England and West Yorkshire. Many have been found in the Long-dendale area on the fringe of the Western Pennines and here, at Mouselow near Glossop, were discovered an extraordinary collection of Celtic Iron Age carved stones in the last century. No-one has been able to decipher their meaning or purpose, although they are believed to have cult significance. Workmen digging foundations for a chapel broke into a kind of collapsed vault containing the stones in 1840. They downed tools and refused to dig. Stored for years, the stones were eventually placed in an archway at Buxton Museum, in their Iron Age exhibition room.

A BBC radio programme broadcast in October 1989 entitled "The Call of the Celts" alleged that, while in storage, the stones prevented the operation of computer equipment in their vicinity and even interfered with an electric typewriter, though both worked perfectly after their removal.

Also a group of people calling themselves the "Guardians of the Old Ways", who seem to belong to an earth veneration cult, claimed to maintain the living embodiment of an oral tradition, handed down in the remote farming communities of Longdendale by their ancient Celtic ancestors. Curiously, place name evidence and archaeological investigation tends to confirm the continuation of a Celtic enclave in Longdendale well into the Saxon period, when it was believed that all the Celts had been driven into Wales, or Scotland. Whether the stones have any significance, the archaeologists are unable to say and it is impossible to assign an exact date to them. However "The Guardians" claim that they know of stone heads buried in the valley near springs and so on whose location is, and remains, their secret.

One of the basic premises of both magic and Christian religion, is the essential ingredient of passion – human, or godlike. Extreme emotion is said to be the spark that jumps the gap between the two worlds – formatory and existing. Therefore the history of many hauntings have some basis in human passion, or tragedy, lost love, suffering, and violent death.

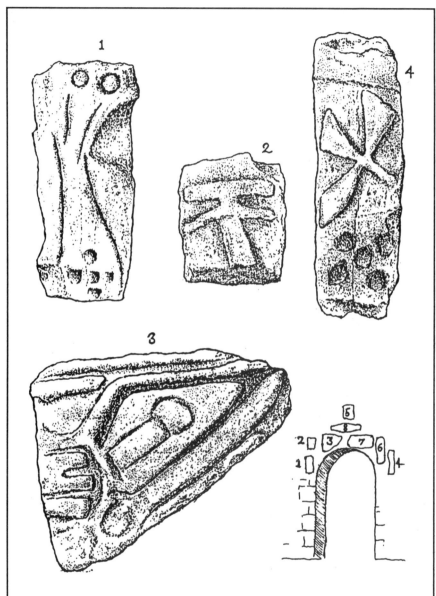

Carved stones found near Glossop in the mid-19th century. Precise origins unknown, but thought to be Celtic (Iron Age) and possibly of cult significance.

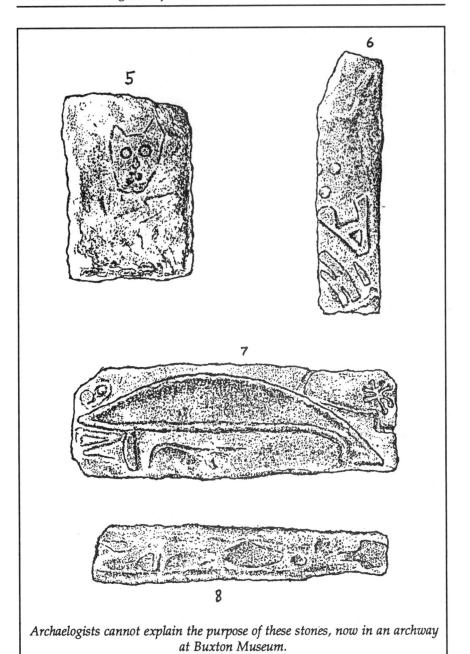

Archaelogists cannot explain the purpose of these stones, now in an archway at Buxton Museum.

We have looked at the case of Samuel Fallows, who was involved in a stormy affair with Betty Shallcross. That he stood trial, and was executed for her murder, is background enough, but the emotions which led up to her murder, and the sufferings she endured, are quite sufficient in the occultists' view of creation to engender the haunting, which apparently still disturbs the neighbourhood of the crime. Their view would be that the crime and emotions attending it would be sufficient to impress an indelible recording on the fabric of the vicinity, so strong, it could continue to influence susceptible people, in the right conditions, possibly indefinitely.

Lethbridge's view of such crimes, and their atmospheres, is even more creepy. He believed that "ghouls" existed in certain places for all time. As a kind of negative energy vortex, they fed on the emotions of humans in their vicinity, acting as a destructive influence. Lethbridge was convinced that they could have been precipitating factors in the case of crimes, and suicides, through affecting the minds of people who happened to come near them, in a receptive state of emotional depression, or instability. What the ghouls were caused by, he couldn't say, but they seemed to be a conglomerate of destructive emotions, and incidents, associated with a certain spot, possibly preserved in the electromagnetic field of a stream, a tree, or rocks.

The fact of objects acting as a focus for paranormal activities has wide credence. Parts of dead people, notably the "screaming skulls" which trigger manifestations when removed from a house, are one example. Another would be objects associated with a violent happening, such as a mirror, splashed with blood, during a murder, which later reflected the scene, to the horror of onlookers.

Although these may seem like good examples of nonsense to the scientific mind, I should like to point out, that even if we take psychology into account, scientific explanation is not sufficient, given the current state of knowledge of psychokinesis, poltergeist hauntings, and in fact hauntings in general, to give any definitive statement on them. To dismiss the lot as rubbish and suggestion, would be the mark of a person who has not researched the subject in any depth, has no real experience of it, and is sadly lacking in a scientific spirit of inquiry.

This is not to say that every tall tale of the paranormal should be accepted as genuine, but each can be examined on its merits.

The main principle of most religions, and indeed, psychic phenomena, is that the manifestations *appear* to proceed from outside, rather than from within the consciousness of the observer. However to paraphrase Jung, everything that proceeds from outside, has first to be filtered on the 'inside' by our own interpretive perception, and related to what we already know, understand, and have experience of, before it reaches us.

That is to say, if we saw a Beutlgrack from the Sirius B planetary system, we would have little, if anything, with which to compare its parts, which made any sense. However the average psychic happening is in a degree familiar. Objects move, sounds are heard, and figures appear – all of which are identifiable, from past, similar, experiences of their "real" equivalents. Real sounds, real objects, real people etc. They could almost be said to have been "created" as dreams are "created" by our unconscious minds every night – or whenever we happen to sleep.

I should like to offer as a *partial* explanation of *some* hauntings, the startling suggestion that, in effect, we *haunt ourselves.*

Most of this chapter has been devoted to showing examples of the very natural human fear of death. It has also given examples of a fear of the dead, and a superstitious desire to placate any vestige of them which many remain, and influence the living. However suppose that the influence which remains, if any, is nothing other than the effect of the memory of the dead person, in those still living, coupled with a fear of the state which had mysteriously transformed them from a moving sentient being, into an inanimate object, which had to be disposed of by burying or burning.

The Rev. Robinson and Mr. Peacock were both afraid of being buried alive. Perhaps the fear of dying is a partial explanation of the fear of ghosts – called by some, telepathically induced hallucinations, and by others, shades of the dead. But perhaps also, the ghosts which haunt us have unpleasant associations with a sense of guilt, of having failed in some way, or a fear of not having done enough for people, as if the dead were, "expecting it of us."

When the living pass over into the realms of inanimate earth in death, they become one with the elements, and in so doing, acquire an almost elemental power, in their ability to influence the imaginations of the living. They haunt the dreams of the living like medieval succubi, the nightriders, producers of nightmares. We all dream at night, but few of us remember of what those night journeys consist.

Whatley Carington said that: "Many psychical phenomena go beyond any explanation that can be offered in terms of the traditional concepts of space and time, matter and energy."

Indeed, space and time are suspended, and become meaningless, in the experiential world of the human psyche during dreams, or in states of trance. Therefore is it surprising that precognitive dreams occur, and clairvoyance gives glimpses at a distance, when these two restrictions no longer impede the pure consciousness of perception?

But what of the figures that rise unbidden from the unconscious mind even when we know that we, "do not dream"? These indeed are spirits – sometimes with all the manifestations of a mighty power, a force which can hurl objects about, reactivate the shades of the dead, suck dry the vital energy of the living – or, turned back on itself, heal the sick, and uplift the hearts of the weary. Jung called it libido – "life force".

Freud in, *The Future of an Illusion* claimed that psychoanalysis had shown that whether God exists or not, there are intensely strong motives in the unconscious impelling a belief in 'Him'. There is a similar irrational desire to accept paranormal phenomena as, "coming from outside oneself", in most people. In a degree, it is true, but not absolutely. The contradiction seems to be that in order to be accepted as genuine "within", the phenomena, religious, or paranormal, must seem to come from "without" the person experiencing it. The ability to rise above the limitations of a personal ego is at the heart of religious experience of a transforming kind. Sometimes great turmoil occurs in the psyche, before this is achieved, and may be projected outside, to external objects and events.

Jung described in detail the inner unconscious world with its archetypal symbolism, frequently reminiscent of mythology. In this world are ghosts, devils, demons, tricksters, birds, snakes, dragons, heroes, and wise old men. A frequent figure in the male unconscious, which crops up in dreams, and waking hypnogogic visions, is that of the anima – a mysterious female, sometimes young, sometimes old, but always with a message to impart.

One of the commonest ghostly phenomena is that of the hauntings by "grey ladies". Few suggestive old mansions are without them. Not many dark and tree-shaded lanes escape their attentions. Whatever the story given to explain their appearance – thwarted love, murder, passions, reclusive eccentricity – they could all be equally well labelled "anima – inspired."

A journalistic friend once described a psychic experience, which he took to be very meaningful. It helped him over a difficult time, and gave him faith that there was more to life than suffering – or beer and skittles.

He was about to have a rather complicated eye operation, the outcome of which would decide his future. He was naturally apprehensive, but just before he was due to go into hospital for the operation he awoke, early one morning, to find the figure of an old lady, in Victorian dress, at the foot of his bed. The apparition smiled, in a kindly way, and said in a soothing voice: "Don't worry, it will be alright." He was greatly relieved, and fell into a blissful slumber. When the operation took place, a few days later, it was a success.

Taken on one level the experience was, as far as my friend was concerned, a genuine paranormal happening. On another level, or looked at from a different angle, it was still a "psychic" happening, but one involving the imparting of a vital message by an anima figure.

I knew another man, approaching middle age, who wove a complicated web of fantasy so inextricably among the strands of his real life, that he could not separate the two. The resulting deception was very difficult for his friends, although he himself was quite happy, and never seemed to notice the embarrassing contradictions in his tales, or even attribute the inevitable financial mess to his own irresponsibility.

One day, he dreamt that he was dozing in bed, when a young woman came running along the landing into his bedroom, jumped into bed with such force, that it bounced him out of bed on the other side. He awoke, startled and confused, standing upright at the side of his bed, which was empty.

He was of the temperament to eagerly seize on ghostly, "explanations", and had no idea what had happened, although he felt it was more real than an ordinary dream, and normally, he didn't remember dreams anyway.

If we ignore ideas of wishful thinking, and bouncing cheques, which were bothering him at the time, and take the female figure as a representation of his unconscious mind, there is a possible explanation. His tendency to fantasise, romance, and involve others in deception, was largely an unconscious function of his personality. He was never really aware that he was "doing it", or at least, never admitted as much to himself, as he was deeply religious. What happened, was that his unconscious was "running away" with him, and he couldn't control it. Most of the time he averted his face from this truth, but when he encountered it, in this cleverly constructed little scenario, he found it frightening, and unacceptable, hence his sudden leap from the bed, when confronting the enormity of his presumption, in the form of a separate entity. At all events, there is no doubt that the figure, and its actions, proceeded from his own psyche, and therefore had a purpose, or personal message to impart. His reaction was to shy away, most clearly demonstrating his normal reaction in life.

Another interesting story of an anima figure is told of Oliver Cromwell. According to his local physician in Huntingdon, Cromwell, when a

young man, was, "splenetic, and full of fancies." He would call out the doctor at all hours of the day and night, convinced that he was dying, and had some odd ideas about the town cross, in Huntingdon. An eminent physician he consulted in London described him as, "very melancholy", which seems to suggest that he suffered from depression.

When still quite young he is said to have seen the figure of a gigantic woman in his bedroom, who told him that he would be, "the greatest man in the kingdom", and that he would be, "close to the King".

Oliver Cromwell – saw apparition

He was later Lord General of the army of Parliament, helped defeat the Royalists, bring the King to trial and execution, and was eventually made Lord Protector, and Head of State, when monarchy was abolished. Enemies attributed his power to witchcraft, and said he was in league with the devil. But, in reality, he was an exceedingly religious and zealous man, with practical gifts. By prayer and meditation it seemed he had access to a finely-attuned instinctive mind of unusual proportions, which led him to take decisions resulting in continual success. An undoubted practical genius, any other explanation would have recourse to 'the hand of God'.

Incidentally, when his brain was removed during autopsy after his death, it was found to be unusually large, and the plentiful blood vessels were said to be, "highly charged". Although no exact correlation between brain size and intelligence has yet been made, it has been alleged that the profusion of blood vessels in the cerebral cortex is important in determining intellect.

After Cromwell's death the Protectorate was soon terminated, and monarchy returned. It is said that three cloaked figures are still seen in the vicinity of Red Lion Square, Holborn, where the bodies of Cromwell, Henry Ireton, and John Bradshaw, were kept overnight, before being taken to Tyburn, and hung up on the gallows as regicides, for the edification of the mob. They had been exhumed from Westminster Abbey, and despite embalming, their funeral wrappings were covered with green mould. Bradshaw, the president of the court who condemned Charles I, was very badly decayed, but eye-witnesses said Cromwell was still recognisable. After hanging all day on the gallows, the corpses were cut down, and the heads hacked off. These were then set on spikes above Westminster Hall, and the bodies thrown into the common lime pit. Cromwell's head eventually blew down in a storm, and was taken away by a sentry. It passed through the ownership of various people, in a semi-mummified state, and was eventually given to his old college, Sidney Sussex, in Cambridge, where, after being photographed, it was given a final, and secret burial.

I heard a story told by an old Lancashire Quaker about Cromwell's final journey. It was a story the old man would often tell his grandchildren, who were brought up in the Quaker tradition that traced its roots back to the turbulent years of the English Civil War. Cromwell's body had been disintered from the Abbey, and taken by cart to the Red Lion, Holborn. There it was to remain all night, until it could be drawn on a hurdle to Tyburn in the morning. The soldiers in charge of the operation were just in the act of man-handling the corpse off the cart, in order to carry it into the inn, when they were terrified by a blood-curdling shriek, followed by peals of cackling laughter. Gathering their wits, and drawing their swords, they looked about, as the baleful corpse lay stiffly, half in and half out of the cart, in its discoloured grave wrappings, and stinking of musty decay.

Another shout attracted their attention to an upper storey window in a house across the street. In the failing light, they could make out a figure, seemingly of an old woman, who leaned out, gesticulating towards them. An unearthly high-pitched voice cut across the gloom:

"You shouldna ha' done it. You shouldna ha' disturbed 'un.

Hae'll nivver rest. Hae'll nivver be able tae rest now!

But hae'll be back tae get you. Hae'll come again!"

And the peals of horrid laughter rang, cackling forth again, in the growing dusk. The soldiers were stunned, and unnerved. Some would have bolted, but the stern command of a sergeant cracked out , and halted them. "Get into that building, and bring her here!" He yelled.

Half a dozen soldiers rushed the place, and searched it from top to bottom, ransacking every room, but not a hide nor hair of any old woman did they find.

"He'll come again!" The old Quaker would repeat, and his grandchildren would interrupt, saying "but he didn't, did he?"

And the old Quaker would smile, and say: "Not yet!"

There are many instances of the appearance of female figures. Some are familiar to the percipient, and some are not. The reverse is equally applicable to animus figures. In the unconscious of women, there is a corresponding male, figure, who may assume many disguises – as her father, her lover, a stranger, or even a religious figure, a saint perhaps. Haunting oneself is a hoary and difficult subject. Animus or anima?

Let us look at some of the subjects we have covered. The case of haunting by demons might be amenable to our explanation. Certainly many of the people who claim to be "possessed" by them, might in fact be possessed by the unacceptable side of their own natures, or something atavistic and brutal, from our animal ancestor past. Primitive tribes very often assume the identity of animals taken as a tribal totem in their ritual dances, dressing in the animal skins, and making noises like them, until they believe themselves to be wolves, hyenas, lions, bears etc. Perhaps there are strong ancestor memories of such primitive cults buried in the deeper layers of our collective unconscious. It is not so very long since two clergymen were severely censured by a judge, for encouraging a disturbed man in his delusional beliefs, by "exorcising" him of scores of demons in one night. They then allowed him out on the street in a dazed and bewildered condition, in which he savagely attacked his wife, tearing off her face with his bare hands. This happened not in the twelfth, but the twentieth century, and not in Borneo, but Barnsley. No doubt there are also "powers", or energies, of the sort we have discussed, which may be handled with extreme care, like dynamite, and for which persons with the expertise of Gurdjieff are required.

Then there are the black magicians – alchemists, as some of them may have been called. Men like the Duke of Buckingham, for whom: "The boasts of heraldry; The Pomp of power; And all that beauty; All that wealth ere gave; Await alike th' inevitable hour. The paths of glory lead but to the grave." And after a rakish, hard-lived life, th' inevitable hour drawing nearer, became his abiding concern, as his alchemical studies consumed all his wealth.

Did he discover the philosophers' stone, and the secret of immortality? Something still seems to linger at the Cock and Bottle, making itself apparent to susceptible individuals. It may all be cock and bottle to say it has anything to do with the Duke. Let alone a stone. Or is it?

The megalithic burial chambers definitely seem charged up with some form of energy. Perhaps it is something to do with them having been paid so much concentrated attention in religious rites and so on, for many ages. Their original purpose may be long forgotten, but the same sun, moon and stars, continue to rise over them, in the same prescribed pattern, following their courses in relation to the megalithic alignments, just as their builders intended. They have a peculiar charisma all their own, similar to that emanating from a good clergyman, just after he has finished conducting a service, in which his activities have been the focal point of attention for his congregation.

The little people, the green men, or fairies, seem partly to be a folk memory of an earlier race, and partly a human perception, and personalisation of a force of nature, which is intuited, or felt. An American author once described how whilst working in the fields in Central America, he was startled to see the happy dancing figure of a little scaly green man, ecstatically giving it the knees up. At the time he had been taking mescaline, from the peyote cactus, and the figure was well known among the Indians as that of Mescalito, the spirit or sprite of the cactus plant. Such awareness of the earth, or vegetation, is not wholly limited to the effect of drugs, although apparently Guinness helps!

The Roman ghosts seem more difficult to explain away. Harry Martindale had no interest in the subject, and he was not the only person to see them. Perhaps in this case a "telepathically induced hallucination" might be the answer. But who were the originators of the "K"s, the original habitual observers of the comings and goings of Roman military life? So much is going on in this strata of psychic activity underneath Treasurers House, ghostly traffic lights could be installed. Is there a leakage of libido, from the religious activity in the nearby Cathedral, powering it all?

Judging by the numbers of ghost stories concerning Roman soldiers, all over the country, it would seem that this era is particularly susceptible to psychic recordings. Perhaps at a deep layer of our ancestral memory there is a strong awe of the Romans still. Their impressive ruined buildings, crowned with ivy, and populated by ghosts, must have been forbidding places to dwellers in halls of wood and thatch, and a constant reminder of vanished imperial glory.

The phenomena associated with the murder of Betty Shallcross, although indistinct, are of the type traditionally ascribed to "disturbed spirits", unable to find contentment, or solace, and doomed forever to pace the scene of the tragedy, fruitlessly covering the same ground. Why this is, and what the imprint is due to, if it exists, other than by suggestion, we can only conjecture. But the phrase, crime of passion, and the views of Lethbridge on extreme, or violent emotions, may be applicable, and have already been discussed.

So what are we to conclude from this catalogue of mystery – a journey into the unknown? We go from cradle to grave with the fundamental meaning of existence hidden from our scrutiny. Science cannot help us here – still grounded, as it is, in Victorian materialism, where the mind is a mere secretion of the brain, and "soul" is poetic licence. The dogma of empirical formulae offers no crumb of comfort, but rather threats of excommunication to the outer darkness of intellectual inadequacy, if we stray too far from accepted doctrine.

Only the inexplicable gives us a glimpse, or a possibility, of there being something beyond materialism. Perhaps if we can bear to look upon the unknown, be it gruesome or sublime, we may see beyond the conflicting opposites, just as Jung predicted, to the land of the inward heart where there be ghosts and goblins, legends and heroes.

To, "the blessed country ever close at hand."

12

SHADOWS UNDER
THE SUN

"The sun wheel is an exceedingly archaic idea, perhaps the oldest that we have. We can trace it to mesolithic and paleolithic stone ages, as early rock drawings in Rhodesia prove. In the Paleolithic Age the actual wheel used in transport had not been invented. The Rhodesian sun wheel is depicted alongside very naturalistic animal pictures, like the rhino with tick-birds. The sun-wheel represents an archetypal sun-image, divided into four or eight partitions. This image, a divided circle, is a symbol which you find throughout the whole history of mankind as well as in the dreams of modern individuals." Jung

The views of Professor Jung on the sun and its motifs are exhaustive and complicated. He adds: "We might assume that the invention of the actual wheel started from this vision."

He also states: "It is the purpose and endeavour of religious symbols to give a meaning to the life man," and quotes an interesting belief of the Pueblo Indians of America which probably reflects the beliefs of earlier peoples elsewhere.

These Indians believe that they are the sons of the Father Sun, and this belief gives their lives a meaning and perspective beyond their individual and limited existence. "It leaves ample room for the unfolding of their personality, and is infinitely more satisfactory than the certainty that one is, and will remain the underdog in a department store," explains Jung. "If St Paul had been convinced that he was nothing but a wandering weaver of carpets, he would not have been himself. His real and meaningful life lay in the certainty that he was the messenger of the Lord. You can accuse him of megalomania, but your opinion pales before the testimony of history and common consensus. The myth that took possession of him, made him greater than a mere craftsman."

The master of ceremonies of the Pueblo Indians told Jung: "Yes, we are a small tribe, and these Americans want to interfere with our religion. They should not do it, because we are the sons of the Father, the Sun. He who goes there (pointing to the sun) – that is our Father. We must help him daily to rise over the horizon, and to walk over heaven. And we don't do it for ourselves only; we do it for America, we do it for the whole world. And if these Americans interfere with our religion through their missions they will see something. In ten years Father Sun won't rise any more, because we can't help him!"

In the morning these Indians arise with a feeling of their great and divine responsibility. They are the sons of the Sun, the Father, and their daily duty is to help the Father over the horizon – not for themselves alone, but for the whole world.

The Indian told Jung: "Look at these Americans. They are always seeking something. They are always full of unrest, always looking for something. What are they looking for? There is nothing to be looked for!"

The Lonan wheelcross, Isle of Man, dating from 450 AD.

Jung agreed, and citing the case of a young woman he met travelling in Africa he drew a curious comparison. She was driving alone from Cape Town to Cairo. "What for?" he demanded. Looking into her eyes he claimed to see the look of a hunted, driven animal. He thought, "if she is killed today nothing has happened, nothing has vanished – because she was nothing!" He considered her to be seeking with no definite aim. Apart from the obvious chauvinism of his viewpoint, which reflected his age and class, Jung's observation is presumptive.

The 8th century "Celtic" cross in Eyam, Derbyshire, with pagan and Christian designs.

But he went on: "If she could say 'I am the daughter of the Moon. Every night I must help the Moon, my Mother, over the horizon.' That makes sense. When people feel they are living the symbolic life, that they are actors in the divine drama, that gives the only meaning to human life!" This is a legitimate viewpoint.

And why is this? Because Jung accepts the sun and moon myths which equate masculinity to one concept and femininity to the other. The sun is the archetypal creator, bringer of day, nourisher of crops, animals and mankind; positive and assertive; it contains within its mystery the secret of birth and death. Moon rules the night, a paler reflection of the sun, it bears the promise of the day to come, within its womb hides the secret of sleep and dreams.

Sun is equated with life, light, warmth and energy. The sun is the self, centre of being in astrology, the essence of one's inner nature, source of libido and growth energy, the outfolding, expanding, expressive quality. It is also love, and love inevitably involves sacrifice, is bound up in nature with suffering, and propitiation of the Gods. Religious sacrifice.

The Pueblo Indians were horrified when Jung suggested that God was not the sun but, "he who made the Sun". "But how can we believe in something we cannot see"? demanded the Indian master of ceremonies. "No, that is our Father whom we see. There is no other behind Him".

There is no other behind Him ...

The world over, sun myths abound. Some are very similar. In the cult of Mithra the sun mounts in his chariot, drawn each day across the heavens representing the sole unconquerable principle, sol invictus, light – "the Sun alone is Absolute". Roman legions worshipped this divinity.

The same myth pertains in Scandinavian mythology, even beyond the twilight of the Gods, after Odin and the old pantheon have passed away in fire and destruction, a new sun, like the one once borne in a chariot across the sky, but devoured by the wolf, Fenris, in the Gotterdamerung, shone serenely, a son of the Sun, in the sky. New gods appeared, free of the blemish and passions that had destroyed the old gods. Balder, fairest of the old Gods, who had gone down to Hell, whom even Odin could not bring back to life, reappeared. Balder the sun god was resurrected. He occupied the great hall where Odin once sat. Men had survived the conflagration. Deep within the world tree, Yggdrasil, which the flames were unable to consume, they had endured. Their only nourishment had been the morning dew.

Frequently the symbol for the sun is a wheel, or a cross imposed on, or within, a sun wheel. Sometimes it is represented otherwise – as a swastika, the three legs of the Isle of Man, as a spiral, or a star – anything implying a spinning motion, movement, and energy.

All mythologies speak of the passage of the sun across the sky. The birth of the sun in the morning is followed by the death, as the sun sinks in the western sky. "The Western Land, land of the setting sun, where sun and land are reunited in an eternally rejuvenating embrace".

In mysticism the inwardly perceived vision of the Divine is often nothing but sun or light and is rarely personified. In Mithraism it was stated that the path of the visible gods, "will appear through the disc of the sun, who is God my Father".

A twelfth century mystic, Hildegarde of Bingen, gave a description of this internal light which is universally typical of such visions. "But the light I see is not local, but is everywhere, and brighter far than the cloud which supports the sun. I can in no way know the form of this light, just as I cannot see the sun's disc entire. But in this light I see at times, though not often, another light which is called by me the living light, but when and in what manner I see this I do not know how to say. And when I see it, all weariness and need is lifted from me, and all at once I feel like a simple girl and not like an old woman".

Jung states: "I am of the opinion that psychic energy, or libido creates the God-image by making use of archetypal patterns, and that man in consequence worships the psychic force active within him as something divine".

He stresses that the image is not "merely" libido and subjectively controlled by consciousness within oneself, but is energy attached to the archetypal symbol, therefore detached from the conscious ego and effectively "outside oneself". One does not control this phenomena, but instead it acts upon us.

The sun therefore is perceived as an external reflection of an internal truth or reality. "One man will derive the idea of God from the sun, another will maintain it is the feelings it arouses which gives the sun its godlike significance".

It remains, however, the undisputed truth that the life-giving sun is a celestial body, without which the earth would be dead rock, if rock is dead, but certainly without what Gurdjieff called the biosphere.

In the water-borne world of the ancient Egyptians, the Western Goddess in the barge of evening gives the sun-disc to the Eastern Goddess in the barge of morning to begin a new day. The rebirth myth of the Egyptians involved the God Osiris, who descends into the tomb, only to conquer death. The God Khepri, a scarab beetle, rolled before him the ball of the sun, as the beetle pushes a ball of dung. To the Egyptians he represented the rising sun, the renewal of life and the idea of eternal existence.

The great Sun God of the Egyptians was Ra.

The religious cults of the world involving the sun are numerous, but that of Ra cast a golden splendour over the mysterious Egyptian pantheon. In the beginning there was Nun, chaos, the primordial ocean in which before the creation, lay the germs of all things and all beings. Texts call him the "Father of the Gods". Inside Nun, before the creation, there had lived a spirit still formless, who bore within him the sum of all existence. This was Atum, and he manifested himself one day as Atum-Ra, Lord of all things, begetter of creation. Ra signifies creator, and is the name of the sun, sovereign lord of the sky. His sanctuary was at Heliopolis, where Ra first manifested in a stone obelisk, preserved in Het Benben, "the palace of the obelisk".

All the gods issued from this one great god who, weary of his own impersonality, in the bosom of the ocean, "rose by an effort of creative will from the abyss".

"From the moment that the sun-god left earth for heaven, his life was immutably regulated. During the twelve daylight hours, he rode in his boat from East to West across his kingdom. During the twelve hours of darkness he passed from cavern to cavern in the underworld, receiving the acclamations of the inhabitants who waited with impatience for the light he bore and after his departure fell back into the agony of darkness".

The Pharaohs called themselves "sons of Ra" because they were born from the union of Ra with the high priest's wife. The gigantic obelisk at Heliopolis was worshiped as a petrified sun's ray. Today there remain only shapeless ruins and the ancient obelisk, the oldest in Egypt, erected to "He who rises in the morning".

One cannot help being struck by the strange energy and power which imbue Egyptian statuary even today. A walk through the galleries of the British Museum's Egyptology section is still an experience on several planes. What did the ancient craftsmen express through their masterly representation of half-human, half-animal deities? By comparison the Assyro-Babylonian statuary is rough and lacking in finesse, the Roman and Greek, posed and humanistic. Stylisation in Egyptian sculpture reached a peak of power and expression through subliminity of its concept, never equalled.

The idea of the "sons of the sun" is a frequent Indian myth. The Aztecs sacrificed the living hearts of men to the sun in their temples. The cult of the sun pervaded Inca life, and there were thousands of temples to the sun throughout their empire. It was believed that their ruler, the Inca himself was directly descended from the sun god. They thought that the sun god, Inti, plunged into the Western Ocean at the end of the day. He returned by swimming under the earth, and reappeared in the morning, rejuvenated by his bath.

Throughout South America and Mexico there is evidence of sun-worship. The Aztecs, like the Incas, adopted many ideas from conquered tribes on the nature of this divinity. The sculpture of the Puerto del Sol, the sun door, carved from a single block of lava on the Bolivian plateau near Lake Titicaca, stands in impressive testimony to the importance of sun-related myths. The stylisation of the reliefs reflect a high level of culture and artistic achievement often seen in sun-based religions, as if the power of the burning disc brought light, warmth and inspiration to the artists and craftsmen of these peoples.

In so many occult and mystic systems of belief the sun occupies a central position, as it does in our solar system, bringing life and light to the earth. In astrology the position of the sun in the natal chart determines the nature of type of the individual. Other aspects, such as position of the other planets and the ascendant are of relative importance to the sun. In the cabala, a mystic system of the ancient Jews, the sun occupied a central position signifying the unified self or essence – much in agreement with Jung's theories of archetypal symbolism. Jung held that the sun signified the God point within oneself.

According to Gurdjieff, the source of the 'ray of creation' was the "Sun Absolute". In our system there was one sun, our sun, and the source of power and energy in our world. Beyond that were all suns or worlds which constituted the "Absolute" or, as he sometimes termed it, God. In his system of belief, energy proceeded from the Absolute through all suns, to their planetary systems, where it was processed according to the immutable laws of the 'ray of creation'.

This involved the intervention of the biosphere, an energy processor, by which finer gradations of matter or energy became coarse, and coarser became fine.

The process by which this occurred was both conscious and intentional and unconscious and automatic. The conscious part involved man and the unconscious the rest of nature, and the natural laws of energy and matter. Man, by certain practices, was capable of transforming the energy into something higher, or alternatively, he could consume it in his normal unconscious automatic processes. Much of this energy was wasted in imagination, or idle day-dreaming, according to Gurdjieff. If the same energy were utilised for a conscious purpose by the practice of self-remembering and the conversion of negative emotions, man had "a career" as Gurdjieff put it, and could "help God".

The concept of sun energy consumed and jettisoned into the stratosphere like so much waste steam, pouring from the heads of idle day-dreamers is a bizarre picture to conjure with.

But what of the priests of old, who worshipped the Sun as Father? Were their efforts of the intentionally conscious kind of which Gurdjieff spoke, and of which he was so definite, holding that all true knowledge was material, and there was only so much of it to go round?

As we have seen in the chapter on megaliths, he believed that knowledge of an objective kind could be stored in physical objects like ancient dolmens, merely awaiting the appropriate means to unlock its secrets.

What happened to these higher gradations of energy? Gurdjieff taught that according to the ancient system of knowledge which he had acquired from Sufi lore, Babylonian and Egyptian mysticism, and an unidentified monastery in the Hindu Kush mountains, it was either returned to the Sun Absolute, or went on to fulfil its role in the evolution of the planetary system, which was conceived as a continually expanding branch, or growing shoot, of the universe. Man, and the whole of nature played an unwitting role in this, as energy transformers, but only man had the chance to use this conversion ability consciously, and in an act of spiritual self-abnegation – by forgoing automatic energy consumption thus helping the Deity by his sacrifice. This act was the act of self-remembering, an almost impossible achievement in a world of sleep where everything "just happens", according to Gurdjieff.

To demonstrate the fact of sleep, Gurdjieff would ask people to describe where they had just been, and what they had seen. Large gaps in memory instantly became apparent.

The sun seems to have played a large part geographically in the psychology of nations. The Japanese describe themselves as living in the land of the rising sun. It is important enough to be a national emblem and appear on flags. Japan is very mountainous, and people living on the West coast are far more likely to see much more of the setting sun. But originally the Japanese came to these islands from the West. They were an offshoot of the Mongols of Northern Asia, and crossed the seas towards these islands "of the rising sun" where they conquered and displaced a more primitive people, the Ainu, who curiously enough worshipped bears. The bears have died out, and so, more or less, have the Ainu. The Japanese, however, have flourished, although their migratory routes are not 'de soleil'.

In China the peoples looked more traditionally toward the West. In Chinese mythology the souls of the just are sent to the Land of Extreme Felicity in the West. This land, which lies in the farthest West portion of the universe, is separated from us by an infinity of worlds like our own. It is a place of all delights where blossoms shower to the ground from trees with 'flowers like gems'. There are lakes with flowering lotuses and banks of golden sand. Birds of many-coloured plumage sing beautifully and the wind in the trees is like music. At the hour of death the just will not be troubled. Buddha himself will receive their souls and place them in the lotuses of the lakes, in which they will remain enclosed until the day comes when, cleansed from all impurities, they escape like fragrance from the opening flower and go to mingle with the just who inhabit the Land of Extreme Felicity in the West.

The Oceanic mythology of the Pacific islanders held that the next world is placed in the West at the point where the sun passes from the sky, either under the earth, or under the sea. In this respect the true West is like the end of the rainbow – impossible to locate, and relative to one's viewpoint. The Pacific islanders believed that in life the body is linked with a different substance, a sort of double, which detaches permanently in death and sets off on its journey to the West, unless, remaining on earth, it becomes a miserable or vindictive ghost, and, on acquiring superior powers, an evil spirit.

This more sinister view is found widely in beliefs of primitive peoples. The dead have to be propitiated, as they envy the living, although, conversely, ancestors were frequently asked for favours in the ritual offerings of the living.

Jung had an interesting idea on the perception of ghosts. He mentioned the importance of the sense of smell in animals. "It is conceivable that intuition in man has taken the place of the world of smells that were lost to him with the degeneration of the olfactory organ". In such a way primitive medicine men "smell" spirits and ghosts. He also gave the example of a man who stayed in an hotel room where he had a dream that a woman had been murdered there. It turned out that the murder had actually happened, unknown to him, days before.

Jung commented: "A dog would surely have smelt the blood, and perhaps recognised it as human, and if he possessed human imagination he would also have been able to reconstruct the essential features of the crime". The human unconscious may well project a visionary picture of the psychic situation that excited it.

The sun is ambivalent. The fertility god is at the same time the destroyer. The sun means fertility and destruction. A lion represents Leo, the zodiac sign of August, standing for the intense heat of the sun, as the rampaging destroying lion. The representation of libido symbolically alternates between the lion and the snake. The principle of dry and wet, according to Jung, opposite sexual or phallic symbols. There are positive and negative embodied in each. Through Christ's death, man is redeemed for eternal life, and a similar idea was expressed in the cult of Mithra. Aion, the sun-god of Mithraism with his lion head and a snake round his body, represents a union of opposites, light and dark, male and female, creation and destruction – the lion symbolising the summer dry time, and the snake the winter wet time. The god has his arms crossed and holds a key in each hand – the keys to the past and the future.

We have already seen how the megalith builders aligned their monuments with the passage of the sun, so that its light illuminated the innermost passages in the depths of winter, at the turn of the year. The Westward movement of the migrations of these people around the Western fringes of Europe, from the Mediterranean, reflects a general trend of movement. Most European peoples migrated at some stage from the East. They were therefore following the setting sun, as we have seen, perhaps on a religious quest for, "the point where the sun leaves the sky", to be nearer their ancestor spirits, and their luck. Their fear is somehow linked with a desire to return "to the source of all things". At night the sun illuminates the land of the dead, and the living are cast into darkness. Like children they wish to be with the Fathers in the light, and long for morning. Like children, they drift after their parents in the West.

The Westernmost land of Europe is Ireland, and some of the most impressive megalithic monuments, with the most splendid stippled ornamentation of Neolithic times are found there. It seems that Ireland, as farthest land of the setting sun was reached comparatively late in the stone age by migrating peoples. The preceding Mesolithic period provides the earliest remains, and it is not apparent that Ireland was settled before this.

In later times the Celtic invasions seem to have supplanted the earlier culture, with a full flowering of traditional Celtic art in metalwork and sculpture. The Druids, whose religious mysteries dominated Celtic society until the coming of the Romans, worshipped the sun and the oak tree, sacrificing to nature and the sun-god, just as the Aztecs of Mexico did centuries later.

Many Irish legends remain, testifying to the potency of older pagan beliefs, but may be attributable to interreligious rivalry between Protestant and Catholic, who each attribute paganism to the other as a reproach, yet still retain a fierce pride in their Celtic roots.

One of the many legends refers to the wheel or circle which, long before the 8th or 9th centuries enclosed the traditional Celtic cross, found in many splendid carvings throughout Ireland and the Celtic fringe of Britain, and also in Scandinavian and Anglican forms throughout England. This wheel is thought to be a Druid symbol signifying the wheel of life. It has also been held to represent a primitive sun wheel, or sun disc, signifying the Son of Man as Christ called himself, or as a Druid symbol of the sun, as the giver of life.

Did the Druids continue to exercise influence so late in the Christian era? The answer seems to be yes. The Druids preached to the Picts of Scotland at the same time as St Columba, who founded the monastic colony of Iona, was trying to convert them to Christianity in about AD 560. Irish missionaries were extremely successful in spreading Christianity in Britain, but they had to contend with paganism from both the Germanic Anglo Saxons and apparently from Celtic sources long after the Christianising Roman influence should have eradicated it. What seems to have happened is that many pagan beliefs and even rituals were incorporated into Celtic Christianity in order for the transition from paganism to take place evenly.

The Celtic wheel-cross reached its finest expression in Irish sculptures frequently containing depictions of complex human and animal figure frescos, carved in relief. It seems to have developed from simple slabs of stone, set upright, like monoliths of the Neolithic era, the surface of which were engraved with simple Christian symbols.

The link with earlier cultures is obvious and may partly be due to the utilisation of convenient remains with an enduring tradition attached to them in folklore and belief.

"The sun wheel is an exceedingly archaic idea, perhaps the oldest that we have. We can trace it to the mesolithic and paleolithic stone ages.. This image, a divided circle, is a symbol which you find throughout the whole history of mankind ... " Jung.

It seems, set at the root of mankind, is a fear, or a belief, linked with an unconscious, or semi-conscious concept of a place, where the "other" people are. We wonder about all those we have known, sometimes friends and relatives, sometimes complete strangers from the deep gallery of history stretching back, endlessly, beyond the grave, who once were, but are no longer with us. Where are they now? Consciously we know the answer. They are dead. Gone. But part of us clings to the irrational, "gone where?" Do they not haunt our dreams, and even our waking moments?

Where is the sun to comfort us? "What light has destiny to guide her little children stumbling in the dark?"

The force of Christianity rebounding from the West like a wave that reaches the farthermost boundary of a distant shore, swept back upon Britain with all the light and power of a sunlit culture. Swept from Ireland, the Westernmost land where the religious luminosity shone brightest in the pagan dark ages, and lit and illuminated the Western world like a lamp or beacon, to aim for, on the farthest promontory of the known world.

Was this the land of the West, "at the point where the sun passes from the sky?"

There are lands, or places of the West, known to be holy from time immemorial, but claimed in later ages as Christian shrines, and all their pagan past forgotten and overlooked. But before we look at them, perhaps we should look at the roots of the Christian Bible itself.

What does the Bible say of the sun? That the sun is a gift of "the Father of the celestial lights" who makes it shine upon all alike, the wicked and the good.

In Acts 26:13 the resurrected Christ presented a light "beyond the brilliance of the sun" in a vision to Paul on the road to Damascus. The day that Jesus was fastened to the cross from eleven in the morning to three in the afternoon a darkness fell over the land "because the sunlight failed" Luke 23:44. This could not have been because of an eclipse of the sun by the moon, as has been suggested, as this was at Passover time which always occurred at the time of the full moon. It is about two weeks later when the moon is new, in the same direction as the sun from the earth – the time when solar eclipses occur.

Jesus stated that the conclusion of the works would see a darkening of the sun.

God was referred to in the Bible as "a sun and shield" as the source of light, life and energy. Divine anger is represented in Revelation 7:16 as the scorching heat of the sun. Jesus said that at the conclusion of the world "the righteous ones will shine as brightly as the sun in the kingdom fo their Father" Matthew 13:39.

Sun worship was resisted by the Israelites, King Josiah put out of business foreign worship involving sacrifices to the sun and moon. He also prevented the horses, which drew a ceremonial chariot dedicated to the sun, from entering the temple, and he had the chariot burned. The prophet Ezekiel had a vision of priests bowing down before the sun in the temple of Jerusalem. This he took as a sign of the forthcoming destruction of the city.

God's "only begotten son", the Word, was a "spirit person" according to one biblical concordance used by a well-known Christian fundamental movement. Existing in "God's form" he later became flesh, residing among man as Jesus. He was put to death in the flesh, but made alive in the spirit. Resurrected, he was glorified alongside the Father with the glory he had possessed in his pre-human state, and God made him "a life-giving spirit" 1 Corinthians 15:45. The Son thus became again invisible to human sight, dwelling "in unapproachable light, whom not one of men has seen, or can see" 1 Timothy 6:14.

The form of spirit is described variously in the Bible to denote spirit as wind "pneuma" or breath "neshama". God is described as having created the natural universe by means of his spirit or active force, "ruah" thus in Genesis 1:2 we read, "God's spirit (ruah) was moving to and fro over the surface of the waters". Neshamah, breath, and ruah, spirit, activate and imbue all living beings with life force. "Breath of the nostrils" seems to be a synonym for a live activated being, "the breath of life" being indissolubly linked in this way with things alive. In the flood, all those creatures on the ground described as having the, "breath of life active in its nostrils" died in the engulfing waters. Psalm 104 says: "If God take away their spirit they expire, and back to their dust they go. "Psalm 146 says that when a man's spirit goes out, "in that day his thoughts perish". When Lazarus was resurrected from the tomb four days after his death he mentioned no conscious state after death. Similarly, Ecclesiastes 12:7 states that at death a person's spirit returns to the true God who gave it".

But what source is this to which the spirit returns?

Some Christian fundamentalists believe that nothing survives death, and describe the returning spirit as mere energy. The only hope of man is in a resurrection of the body, by the return of the life-giving, energizing spirit in a reconstituted physical self, which God has the power to make.

That which returns to the Father (or the Sun, in some cults) is the spirit energy which activated the life force in the living body. This idea bears some resemblance to Gurdjieff's teaching that energy returns to the Sun Absolute or is consumed by the moon, which he sometimes equated with the Devil. Energy going to the sun, according to Gurdjieff, was recycled, but that going to the moon was trapped there, along with, "perhaps some remnant of consciousness", in the human "souls" thus imprisoned. Shades of Hades!

A Celtic Hades existed in the domain of King Nudd, or Gwyn ap Nudd, Lord of the dead, and King of the fairies or little people. This Nudd was a strange being, depicted as a Youth, the leader of wild hunts in the night sky, and having some correlation with Odin or Woden in that respect. It was said that he had a castle on the summit of Glastonbury Tor, the strange stump of land which arises from the surrounding marshes, and described by some as the fabled Avalon, whence the dying Arthur was taken to mend his wounds.

Many have regarded this Somersetshire spot as the spiritual centre of Britain. It was probably holy in pre-Christian times because a story is related of the Welsh saint Collen. Invited to the castle on top of the Tor, Collen was received by Nudd, but declined to eat or drink the fairy food he was offered. When he suddenly hurled holy water over the assembled company, King, damsels, minstrels and castle all disappeared, leaving him alone on the grassy knoll.

Nudd is thought to be the same as the ancient British Nodens, a god of healing and the Irish Nuada, but his Lordship of the dead is specifically a Welsh idea, relating fairy people to demons who preside over the land of Annwn, according to Geoffrey Ashe, a marshalling place of departed souls, akin to the legendary Avalon.

Dion Fortune, the occultist, felt that the spiral pathway to the summit of the Tor was further proof of its pagan origins. Such places, she alleged were always sacred to the sun.

At the foot of the Tor is the chalice well. Here a yew stump adjacent to the stones of the well was dated by carbon analysis back to Roman times. It is known that wells formed an essential part of Mithraic ritual in Roman worship of the solar deity. The later Christian symbology of the Holy Grail may have been grafted on an earlier form of religion. A religion of the sun.

Another "land of the West" celebrated in Christian mysticism is Iona. Its Gaelic name, Innis-nam-Druidbneach, island of the Druids, confirms its earlier importance in an older religion. After Columba, it was Christianised to all appearances. Its strong atmosphere continues to attract more than just Christian visitors, as does Glastonbury. A strangely-shaped hill, Sithean Mor, on the West of the island, traditionally a "fairy" mound, was the last place on earth visited by a friend of Dion Fortune, who performed a magical ritual there at night, to access the elemental energies. In the morning, she was found dead, a fact widely reported in the newspapers. Curiously, Christian scholars claim this as the spot that St Columba also "met the angels". What the Druids did here, and possibly the megalith builders before them, we do not know.

Certainly, stone circles built by ancient peoples are still known in Gaelic as Bel Beachd – the circle of Bel, the Celtic sun god. Beltane, the summer festival was celebrated in Scotland's Western Highlands as late as the eighteenth century. Country people would walk sunwise, three times around cairns or monuments to obtain good fortune, and various other sun-related "superstitions" abound.

The circle of stones at Callanish, on the island of Lewis, are thought to be another sun-temple with the added distinction of being the last Druid site ever used. Alleged to be the "great winged temple of the Northern Isles" mentioned by the Greek, Herodotus, it has a central monolith seventeen feet in height, and consists of eighteen stones at present, although formerly it was much larger, having separate wings of stones. The atmosphere here is credited with various properties, including the ability to cure toothache!

Shrines and temples to the sun, fairy mounds, lordship of the dead, lands of the West – tenuous connections perhaps, and puzzling. What do they mean?

Primitive peoples, if ever a people could be described as such, held the sun and moon to be heavenly divinities. The sun represented warmth and day, and the moon the cool light of night. Throughout the world they are regarded in myth and legend as a twin godhead, always the sun is male, the moon, the female aspect of divinity.

As the positive and assertive life-giver, the sun was pursued in the early migrations of people. Going "sunwise", in the direction of the sun, was held to be a holy rite, incumbent on those who wished to be attuned to the great cosmic plan. Since most energy appears to come from the sun, who can state conclusively that these "primitive" views are mistaken. Man has yet to travel beyond the stars. Or away from his own solar system.

But the psychology of the parallel is clear. Man is both mortal and immortal. His body faces death and dissolution, but that immortal part of him which can survive, is that which comes from, and belongs to, the sun – either figuratively, or literally depending on one's religious belief. The symbolism is clearly that the setting sun represents man's mortality. But the plunge into the depths, or the rejuvenating waters of the sea, results in rebirth – the sun is born again in the morning as the rising sun, the ever-immortal aspect of the solar deity.

To arrive at the place of arising, or rebirth, one has to go with the setting sun – to the West.

Jung stated: "The sun comparison tells us over and over again that the dynamic of the gods is psychic energy ... This is our immortality. The psychic life force, the libido, which symbolises itself in the sun".

Perhaps it is no accident that the early Christian symbol was that of a fish. Capricorn is represented as a being with the body of a goat, and the tail of a fish. It rules that period of the year when the sun mounts from the depths of winter on its summerward path, in January. As a turning point, its symbolism shows how the goat climbs to the highest point of the mountains, only to plunge into the deepest depths of the sea, as a fish. So too, the sun climbs heavenward, only to plunge again for its rejuvenating bath in the ocean.

The fish therefore represents rebirth, and renewal of the life force, and is connected in this way with the concept of the solar deity. Its frequent appearance in dreams is borne out by such symbolism and shows an unsuspected Christian esotericism. Christ was described as "a fisher of men" and as such brings them to rebirth, and renewal in life, and the hope of resurrection beyond it. The Druids also worshipped a deity known as "the Fisher King".

We have come a long way from ghosts, which provide shadowy evidence of human belief in another existence, along with demons and fairies which may or may not have arisen from a primitive fear of the dead returning. It must often have been the case that those apparently dead did revive, to the fear and consternation of the mourners.

Perhaps our point of departure should be a reflection on this tale told by Jung of a simple African people. After playing happily in the dust for some time, a young negro pointed to his shadow. "You see that man down there?" he asked Jung. "When I die, my body goes down into the earth, where he is. But he goes up, into the sun. And he lives forever."

POSTSCRIPT

Since I wrote this work I have met and talked with other investigators into the psychic realms whose views differ from my own. In place of their cut and dried beliefs I maintain a degree of scepticism.

Having visited many "haunted" sites and listened to witnesses of "phenomena" I can definitely state that the vast majority of supernatural reportings are based on misobservation, bad eyesight, suggestibility, exaggeration and so on. It is when all logical possibilities are ruled out, that a case becomes interesting.

I have never seen and expect that I never will observe an apparition, but would be quite pleased to do so should the opportunity arise. My "K" rating is perhaps too low. I do however believe that I have shown the objective existence of energies presently unrecognised by science, but which may have no relation to persons who have departed this life. Such energy seems to be an attachment of the living and perhaps it is best kept that way. Most things in nature have their opposites.

When my father died unexpectedly and I was called to identify him, I could clearly see from several yards away that the waxen form on the mortuary trolley had lost all that constituted him in life, just a couple of hours before. When I touched his shoulder he was still warm, but neither sentiment nor sense could induce me to believe that a trace of him remained. I knew that, to misquote Marvell, "from that leaden slumber he would wake no more".

To salve my conscience I attended a spiritualist circle before the funeral – in case of the slightest possibility of a message. No-one knew why I was there, I had never been before, or of the death of my father. The first message the medium produced was from an impatient gentleman, "whose heart went pop, and he rushed into the world of the spirit", to quote her words. The message was trite enough, "everything will be all right". It was not directed by her to me, but the circumstances she described fitted those of my father's death. A coincidence? Maybe. But he was the only heart attack victim she got a message from that night.

FURTHER READING

Bibliography

A Step in the Dark: T C Lethbridge, Routledge and Kegan Paul, 1967

Circles and Standing Stones: Evan Hadingham, Heinemann, 1975

Beyond Stonehenge: Gerald S Hawkins, Hutchinson, 1973

Ancient & Historic Monuments of the Isle of Man: Manx Museum & National Trust, 1981

Wales - Castles & Historic Places, Wales Tourist Board, 1980

Mysterious Wales: Chris Barber, Granada, 1983

Report of the Trial of Samuel Fallows: Stockport Advertiser, 1823

Dr Robinson's Grave: Stockport Heritage Magazine, 1991

Ghosts of an Ancient City: John Mitchell, (pub. John Mitchell) York 1974

Secret Talks with Mr G, IDHHB Inc., 1978

In Search of the Miraculous: P D Ouspensky, Routledge and Kegan Paul, 1950

The Collected Works of C G Jung: Routledge and Kegan Paul

Synchronicity - An acausal connecting principle: C G Jung, Routledge and Kegan Paul

Secret of the Golden Flower: Richard Wilhelm & C G Jung, Routledge and Kegan Paul

Witness: John G Bennett, Turnstone Books, 1974

General References

Chambers Encyclopedia

Encyclopedia Britannica

Journal of the Society for Psychical Research

Encyclopedia of World Mythology

Concordance of the Holy Bible

This list is not exhaustive and is intended for guidance only

Index

We publish a wide range of titles, including general interest publications, guides to individual towns, and books for outdoor activities centred on walking and cycling in the great outdoors throughout England and Wales. This is a recent selection:

General interest:

THE INCREDIBLY BIASED BEER GUIDE – Ruth Herman
This is the most comprehensive guide to Britain's smaller breweries and the pubs where you can sample their products. Produced with the collaboration of the Small Independent Brewers' Association and including a half-price subscription to The Beer Lovers' Club. *£6.95*

DIAL 999 – EMERGENCY SERVICES IN ACTION – John Creighton
Re-live the excitement as fire engines rush to disasters. See dramatic rescues on land and sea. Read how the professionals keep a clear head and swing into action. *£9.95*

THE ALABAMA AFFAIR – David Hollett
This is an account of Britain's rôle in the American Civil War. Read how Merseyside dockyards supplied ships for the Confederate navy, thereby supporting the slave trade. The *Alabama* was the most famous of the 'Laird Rams', and was chased half way across the world before being sunk ignominiously. *£9.95*

PEAK DISTRICT DIARY – Roger Redfern
An evocative book, celebrating the glorious countryside of the Peak District. The book is based on Roger's popular column in *The Guardian* newspaper and is profusely illustrated with stunning photographs. *£6.95*

I REMAIN, YOUR SON JACK – J. C. Morten (edited by Sheila Morten)
A collection of almost 200 letters, as featured on BBC TV, telling the moving story of a young soldier in the First World War. Profusely illustrated with contemporary photographs. *£8.95*

FORGOTTEN DIVISIONS – John Fox
A unique account of the 1914 – 18 War, drawing on the experience of soldiers and civilians, from a Lancashire town and a Rhineland village. The book is well illustrated and contains many unique photographs. *£9.95*

ROAD SENSE – Doug Holland
A book for drivers with some experience, preparing them for an advanced driving test. The book introduces a recommended system of car control, based on that developed by the Police Driving School. Doug Holland is a highly qualified driving instructor, working with RoSPA. *£5.95*

Books of Walks:

There are many books for outdoor people in our catalogue, including:

RAMBLES IN NORTH WALES
– Roger Redfern

HERITAGE WALKS IN THE PEAK DISTRICT
– Clive Price

EAST CHESHIRE WALKS
– Graham Beech

WEST CHESHIRE WALKS
– Jen Darling

WEST PENNINE WALKS
– Mike Cresswell

STAFFORDSHIRE WALKS
– Les Lumsdon

NEWARK AND SHERWOOD RAMBLES
– Malcolm McKenzie

NORTH NOTTINGHAMSHIRE RAMBLES
– MAlcolm McKenzie

RAMBLES AROUND NOTTINGHAM & DERBY
– Keith Taylor

RAMBLES AROUND MANCHESTER
– Mike Cresswell

WESTERN LAKELAND RAMBLES
– Gordon Brown

WELSH WALKS:
Dolgellau and the Cambrian Coast
– Laurence Main and Morag Perrott

WELSH WALKS:
Aberystwyth and District
– Laurence Main and Morag Perrott

MOSTLY DOWNHILL:
Leisurely walks in the Lake District
– Alan Pears

WEST PENNINE WALKS
– Mike Cresswell

– all of the above books are currently £6.95 each

CHALLENGING WALKS IN NORTH-WEST BRITAIN
– Ron Astley *(£9.95)*

WALKING PEAKLAND TRACKWAYS
– Mike Cresswell *(£7.95)*

Long-distance walks:

For long-distance walks enthusiasts, we have several books including:

THE GREATER MANCHESTER BOUNDARY WALK
– Graham Phythian

THE THIRLMERE WAY
– Tim Cappelli

THE FURNESS TRAIL
– Tim Cappelli

THE MARCHES WAY
– Les Lumsdon

THE TWO ROSES WAY
– Peter Billington, Eric Slater,
Bill Greenwood and Clive Edwards

THE RED ROSE WALK
– Tom Schofield

FROM WHARFEDALE TO WESTMORLAND:
Historical walks through the Yorkshire Dales
– Aline Watson

THE WEST YORKSHIRE WAY
– Nicholas Parrott

– all £6.95 each

The Best Pub Walks!

Sigma publish the widest range of "Pub Walks" guides, covering just about every popular walking destination in England and Wales. Each book includes 25 – 30 interesting walks and varied suitable for individuals or family groups. *The walks are based on "Real Ale" inns of character and are all accessible by public transport.*

Areas covered include

Cheshire • Dartmoor • Exmoor • Isle of Wight • Yorkshire Dales • Peak District • Lake District • Cotswolds • Mendips • Cornwall • Lancashire • Oxfordshire • Snowdonia • Devon

… and dozens more – all £6.95 each!